PICNIC BASKET

Elizabeth Kent has been a keen cook for many years. Her culinary skills and varied repertoire were acquired while living abroad in France, Switzerland and North America. Her home is now in London from where she writes a syndicated cookery column for a large newspaper group. She is also the author of several books for children, one of them on cookery.

ELIZABETH KENT

PICNIC BASKET

'Then from his knapsack very calmly and contentedly he takes cold chicken and golden encrusted rolls, packed for him perchance by loving hands, and lays conveniently by the wedge of Gruyère or Roquefort which is to be his whole dessert.'
Brillat Savarin

FONTANA BOOKS

First published in Fontana 1978

Copyright © Elizabeth Kent 1978

Made and printed in Great Britain by
William Collins Sons & Co Ltd, Glasgow

Set in Monotype Times

To everyone at Fontana –
who sampled picnic after picnic
without complaint

The Author and Publishers would like to thank the following for permission to reprint copyright material:

John Murray (Publishers) Ltd and Sir John Betjeman for the extract from the latter's *Collected Poems*; to the Estate of P. G. Wodehouse for the extract from the latter's *Jeeves and the Old School Chum*; to Curtis Brown Ltd, Charles Scribner's Sons Inc. and the Estate of Kenneth Grahame for the extract from *Wind in the Willows*; to David Higham Associates, Michael Joseph Ltd and Elizabeth David for the extract from the latter's *Summer Cooking*; to Hamish Hamilton Ltd and the Estate of L. P. Hartley for the extract from *The Go-Between*; to Chatto and Windus Ltd and Mrs Joan Lindsay for the extract from the latter's *Picnic at Hanging Rock*; to Edward Arnold Publishers Ltd and the Estate of E. M. Forster for the extract from *A Passage to India*; to J. M. Dent and Sons Ltd and Constance Spry for the extract from *The Constance Spry Cookery Book*; to The American Heritage Publishing Company for the extract from *The American Heritage Cookbook*; to David Higham Associates, Macmillan Publishers Ltd and Frank Magro for the extracts from Osbert Sitwell's *Sing High! Sing Low!*; to Farrar, Straus and Giroux Inc. for the extract from L. M. Montgomery's *Anne of Green Gables*.

With special thanks to the following picnic experts:

Helen, Ginnie, Giles, Robert, Lorna, John, Anthony, Lizzie, Will, Georgie, Peter, Anne – Nigel, David and Jeanette.

CONTENTS

ALL TABLESPOON AND TEASPOON MEASUREMENTS ARE LEVEL
UNLESS OTHERWISE SPECIFIED.

INTRODUCTION

It may be possible to refuse a dinner, a brunch or an invitation to tea; but never a picnic. For the idea of a feast outdoors, with the finest food and company, is usually irresistible. However cold and wet the last one might have been, the prospect of another is always viewed with fresh hope. Even threatening storm clouds and a sudden drop in temperature cannot mar the anticipation. This time it will be different: the sun will come out, the ants will vanish and the lemon meringue pie will stay in one piece.

Regardless of the season, a picnic provides a perfect excuse for city-dwellers to escape to the country and for country-dwellers to explore it further. It can be a pretext for lying by the riverside all day reading a book or it can be eaten en route to a session of bird-watching or collecting wild flowers. You might be in a rowing boat, at the racecourse, half-way up a mountain or flying a kite.

Gourmets and 'gourmands' might be unwilling to describe a picnic as a gastronomic adventure but that, by varying degrees, is what it is. It has all the classic ingredients: the suspense of not knowing on a seaside picnic whether the tide is coming in or going out; the drama of forgetting the corkscrew; the thrill of eating on a cliff-edge, and the unpopular surprise ending of a torrential downpour. A picnic has, undoubtedly, a sense of excitement which no meal indoors can lay claim to.

There must have been excitement of quite a different kind when the 'pic nic' first made its appearance in this country. Coming via France (where 'pique-niques' were already well known) and Germany ('Picken und Nicken'), the word was used about 1800 to refer to a 'harmless and inoffensive society of persons of fashion'. Known as 'The Pic Nic Society', they performed theatricals, concerts and other social entertainments to which all members contributed. It seems to have been a popular idea for the word soon spread to other activities. The

Annual Register of 1802 reports that 'This season has been marked by a new species of entertainment, common to the fashionable world called a Pic Nic supper.' Details of such an occasion are provided by *The Times* (16 March 1802): 'A Pic Nic Supper consists of a variety of dishes. The Subscribers to the entertainment have a bill of fare presented to them, with a number against each dish. The lot he draws obliges him to furnish the dish marked against it, which he either takes with him in his carriage, or sends by a servant.'

The contributory nature of a picnic is still one of its highlights, provided everyone doesn't turn up with the same thing. It needs to be well organized without spoiling the spontaneity. Otherwise you might end up with plenty of food, but no plates or cutlery. If the cutlery *is* forgotten, the younger picnickers (who would like to do away with it altogether) will be delighted. Eating with fingers always adds to the fun and guarantees the informality of the occasion. Part of the attraction is that anything small enough to be eaten with fingers can also be slipped into a pocket. This makes a more portable picnic and as Winnie-the-Pooh points out, carrying 'a little something' on every outing is sure to come in handy.

The advantages of eating outdoors are numerous and often underrated. For one, there is much greater leeway in the presentation and 'delivery' of the food than would ever be allowed at a meal indoors. This is a great boon to the last-minute or inexperienced chef. If the quiche lorraine, through some mishap, becomes quiche crumble, then no one looks the slightest bit surprised. It is devoured regardless and the hostess is complimented on her ingenuity. Sloping sponge cake is another example. Whereas its arrival on the Sunday lunch table might be greeted with giggles, it looks completely natural on the uneven surface of a picnic tablecloth.

Fresh air is the picnic's greatest asset. Its revitalizing effect on appetites and food causes both to improve dramatically. Like pulling rabbits from a hat, anything produced from the picnic basket seems like a miraculous culinary feat. Everything tastes exceptionally good, better than it ever has done before. And the same meal, eaten in the Bois de Boulogne, Kew Gardens and at Land's End, will taste different each time.

A picnic also allows you the freedom of deciding when, where and *how* you will eat. If you feel like dangling your feet in a cool brook while munching a sandwich, you can do. No one expects you to sit up straight and not a single eyebrow will be raised if you eat a pork pie lying in a horizontal position. You can even adopt a more unusual posture, as Francis Kilvert describes in his *Diary* (1870–9):

> . . . we joined the Truro Hockins and a party of their friends for a picnic down the river . . . We rowed or rather were rowed by boatmen down to Tregothnan . . . we walked up to the house, and down the other hill to the boat house, just above which we had tea all across the road completely obstructing the thoroughfare. Our hostess reclined gracefully on her side up the slope of a steep bank and thus enthroned or embedded dispensed tea and *heavy* cake and was most hospitable.
>
> . . . I unhappily mistook butter for cream (Tell it not in Truro) and was much concerned about our hostess lest she roll down the bank into the river. Also I was exceedingly puzzled to find out how it was she did not so roll, for *what was to hinder it?*

Finding the right picnic spot is not always as easy as it might appear. Trollope (whose 'Marine Picnic' features later in the book) insists that 'a picnic must be held among green things. Green turf is absolutely an essential. There should be trees, broken ground, small paths, thickets and hidden recesses. There should, if possible, be rocks, old timber, moss and brambles. There should certainly be hills and dales . . .' In *David Copperfield*, Dickens describes a picnic which takes place in 'a green spot, on a hill, carpeted with soft turf. There were shady trees, and heather, and, as far as the eye could see, a rich landscape.' While this sounds ideal, when searching for picnic spots of similar description, they can be remarkably elusive. But happily, the number of successful meals in caves, on barren clifftops and mid-Channel prove that these attributes are not *absolutely* essential.

The inherent differences between meals indoors and out are ones which merry-makers might not at first be aware of. Mrs Beeton, in a late-nineteenth-century edition of *Every Day Cookery*, draws these to the readers' attention:

> Little mistakes will invariably occur at all picnics that are not ceremonious ones; things will be forgotten; some viands possibly spoilt by bad packing, and such like small troubles; but these are nothing compared to the mistakes of bringing the wrong people together, of placing without regard for individual tastes in the vehicles used, or having too many of one sex in the party. At a picnic there is no get-away for any-one, as there is at an evening party or an 'at home'. However dull and bored one may feel, one must stay to the bitter end of these al fresco entertainments.

This is something which *hasn't* changed since Victorian times.

The weather hasn't changed either. It is still as unpredictable as ever. Though this preserves an element of surprise, it does make planning difficult. As soon as a picnic is arranged, a gloomy forecast is inevitably issued for the same day. But what satisfaction when the experts are proved wrong and the picnic is bathed in sunshine and warmth!

Intrepid picnickers thrive on eating outdoors all year round. But, on the whole, there seems to be little rush to follow their example. Winter picnics, though many may be surprised to hear it, can be just as enjoyable as summer ones. Warming up with Glühwein and later lunching on hot pies and soup is exhilarating. Spring picnics are best eaten on a mossy riverbank, just as the daffodils are coming out. A basket filled with local produce and a bottle of unchilled white wine make a delectable March meal. In the summer, picnics should be as light and lazy as possible. Pack lots of crisp, crunchy salads, cold punch and ice-cream, then savour them while punting down-river or on an island with a cool breeze. In the autumn, a bonfire picnic is the best. Roast sausages, cider, rosy apples and thick slabs of gingerbread are all you need.

Fishing and shooting picnics are among the most traditional and they share one thing in common: the participants are, without exception, more interested in the sport than in the food. The ideal picnics for them are ones which can be packed, carried and eaten with the minimum of fuss and bother. In a Victorian cookbook (Lady Harriet St Clair's *Dainty Dishes*, 1862), we find the following advice for a shooting breakfast: 'Gentlemen usually prefer eating this about the middle of the day, in the open air, with their fingers, in order that they may lose no time; so it is not generally necessary to send knives and forks or tablecloths; but you must take care, in order not to make them angry, that the luncheon is there at the right time and place.'

With hours of picnicking pleasure ahead, it comes as some relief to know that the tradition is planted in solid ground. Osbert Sitwell, in his essay *Picnics and Pavilions*, leaves us confident that, whatever happens, the future of picnics is assured:

Particularly in times of great wickedness and folly, the contemplation of so idyllic, so simple a delight holds a particular poignancy; yet of one thing you can be sure; whether or no the picnic is a true pleasure, the habit of it is so firmly engrained in human character that it will survive countless calamities and holocausts.

1

PLANNING PICNICS

'Things not to be Forgotten at a Picnic'

A stick of horseradish, a bottle of mint sauce well corked, a bottle of salad dressing, a bottle of vinegar, made mustard, pepper, salt, good oil, and pounded sugar. If it can be managed, take a little ice. It is scarcely necessary to say that plates, tumblers, wine-glasses, knives, forks and spoons must not be forgotten; as also teacups and saucers, 3 or 4 teapots, some lump sugar, and milk, if this last-named article cannot be obtained in the neighbourhood.

from *Mrs Beeton's Book of Household Management* (1861)

Why is it that the 'perfect picnic' is always organized by someone else? When left to do it on one's own, there seem to be more things forgotten than remembered. The most delectable item is inevitably left behind while the stale fruit-cake turns up without fail. Corkscrews go missing so often that one begins to suspect a conspiracy by the Temperance Society. Tin-openers are equally guilty for when they *do* put in an appearance, it's usually to prove they don't work. Favourite picnic grounds must by now be layered in lost cutlery, last seen in the long grass. But the worst predicament of all must be that suffered by the Three Men in a Boat* when not one but two crucial items are forgotten. This is enough to drive even the most stable picnicker to his knees.

There are several ways of combating this absentmindedness:

* See Chapter 12.

some more successful than others. If the picnic is arranged 'au style sergeant-major', then everything is organized with military precision. Rations of food and drink are handed out with such speed that if slow to sit down, one could miss out altogether. Or, if you prefer, it can all be done according to 'The List'. This very simple manœuvre of packing by name and number is one that many people swear by (which is what the others do when they forget it). If done properly, this method is second to none for getting all the right things into the basket. Getting them all back in again after the picnic is another matter altogether.

To spare the picnicker any future anguish over the 'incomplete' nature of his meal outdoors, the following lists have been compiled. They have been deliberately fashioned to generous proportions so that if one or two items fail to turn up, the results should not be too dramatic.

Picnic Equipment

Picnic Basket or Hamper

There is always something special about a picnic which arrives in a wicker basket. It may be the association with Edwardian picnics that makes one anticipate an eight- or nine-course feast by Mrs Beeton. Or it could be the connection with the country that makes one feel the basket must be brimming with the freshest and the best home-made food (an insulated bag doesn't seem to hold quite the same promise). If searching for a good picnic basket, look for one with a level bottom. Those with a circular or uneven pattern will send everything you put on top of it sliding to one side or other. Make sure, too, that the basket itself is not too heavy or you'll need a crane to lift it when filled. Check that the handle is securely fixed. Hampers are now being made with handles at each end so that they can be carried flat and not sideways in the traditional manner. This prevents the inevitable happening: the stuffed eggs sliding on to the strawberry flan the moment the hamper is picked up.

Tablecloth or Picnic Rug

If taking a tablecloth, it should be a fairly heavy one so that you don't spend your time chasing it down a windy field. It is infinitely preferable to a picnic rug during the summer as it is cool and has none of the itchiness of wool. Avoid, if you can, using plastic tablecloths if it's very hot as you'll find everything sticks to them, including the guests. But the picnic rug is indispensable during the winter, providing warmth and protection from the damp ground. Both tablecloth and rug can double as insulators: see the section on Packing.

Insulated Bags and Boxes

These are marvellous for transporting food and keeping it at the right temperature. They are either made in firm plastic in the shape of a box or in a lightweight plastic material made into a soft-sided bag with straps. There are also insulated ice buckets which are useful when making cold punches and catering for large numbers. All of these can be found in the picnic or camping sections of large department stores.

Thermos Flasks

Most ironmongers and department stores carry a wide range of Thermos flasks in varying sizes. The latest wide-necked ones will keep food hot or cold up to six hours (and sometimes longer). They do, unfortunately, vary according to the manufacturer and some are considerably better than others, so do read the labels and ask the advice of a sales assistant before buying. The tall, thin Thermos is still the most popular for drinks and soups and usually carries a larger quantity than the short kind. Both should be prepared properly before filling: see the sections on Keeping Food Hot and Cold.

Ice-Packs

These are made in strong, sturdy plastic and once frozen can be put under, on top of or around food that needs to be kept chilled. They will stay frozen up to four hours, depending on the weather. (Available from ironmongers and department stores.)

Plastic Cups, Glasses, Plates

Remarkable strides forward have been made recently in plasticware and the glasses especially have been greatly improved. Cups, bowls and plates are now being produced in matching colours and, though still rather expensive, they are long-lasting.

Plastic Cutlery

Though still far from ideal, these are a lot less painful to lose in the sand or over the side of a boat than the best family silver.

Paper Plates and Cups

A godsend when it comes to washing-up, these can now be found in attractive colours and designs. Some have a laminated surface which makes them stronger and reusable. But do use them with care; they are never as sturdy as china or plastic plates and are liable to collapse under the weight of a heavy cheesecake.

Lightweight Salad Bowl

Until recently, the weight of wooden salad bowls made taking them on a picnic practically impossible. But now lightweight ones are being made in various sizes (and at reasonable prices). Plastic salad bowls have been available for some time and usually come in colours to match a range of bowls, plates, etc. Salad utensils can be found either in a lightweight wood or in plastic.

Plastic Containers and Biscuit Tins

Collect these in all shapes and sizes. The plastic containers are especially good for keeping food moist, while the tins are better for anything that needs to be kept crisp (biscuits, melba toast, etc.). Make sure when you put the lid on a plastic container that it is on straight, otherwise it will warp. The see-through plastic containers with colourful lids are ideal for transporting and serving food on a picnic and can also double as storage jars.

Aluminium Foil Containers

These, normally associated with take-away food, are useful for packing and keeping food hot. If wrapped in layers of damp newspaper or tea towels or packed in an insulated bag, they will retain the heat for several hours.

Polythene Bags

These are invaluable when it comes to packing for a picnic and a supply of various weights and sizes is always handy. The large rubbish-bin size can be used to line the basket, to put under the picnic rug as protection against the damp ground and, finally, to put rubbish in at the end of the picnic. The smaller sizes are practical for wrapping cutlery, salt and pepper, ice-packs, etc., as well as food.

Cling Film

A real boon to the picnicker, this is excellent for keeping food fresh and moist. It will stick to most dishes and containers but if, for some reason, it doesn't, secure it with Sellotape. It is remarkably strong and you can stack containers covered with it on top of each other with little fear of them collapsing. It also makes it easy to see at a glance what a bowl contains.

Foil

A necessity at barbecue and camping picnics and extremely useful at any other. It won't stick to food in the same way that cling film will (its one drawback) and so should be used with anything that has a glaze or sticky surface (e.g. an iced cake or a pâté covered with aspic jelly). It can also protect fragile items like cakes, flans or raised pies during the journey. (Simply crumple a piece of foil, roll it up loosely and carefully put round the pie, keeping it about an inch from it all around.) This will give it some protection against jolts or against other containers sliding into it. For cooking, the heavy-duty foil is best as it doesn't tear as easily as the ordinary kind.

Bubble Wrap

This recent invention is used to wrap fragile stereo parts or fine china. Don't throw it away as it is extremely good for insulating food, either hot or cold. Wrap it round the food (put it in a container or wrap in foil first), secure with Sellotape, and it will keep it warm (or cold) for several hours.

Absorbent Kitchen Paper

This can be used as a tablecloth or napkins (if either of these fail to materialize) and for last-minute repairs to the food, wiping up spills, etc.

Paper Napkins

These now come in a wide range of colours and textures. They are very versatile and can be used to line small serving baskets, wrap cutlery or sharp knives and give a bright splash of colour to the picnic food.

J-Cloths

Dampened and carried in a plastic bag, these are indispensable when it comes to mopping up, cleaning sticky fingers, etc.

Extras

The list could be endless, depending on personal tastes, but a large umbrella, matches, drinking water and a torch are essential.

Picnic Check List

Plates
Glasses
Cups
Bowls
Forks/spoons/knives
Serving spoons
Sharp knives for slicing bread and cheese
Napkins
Corkscrew/bottle-opener/ tin-opener

Salt and pepper
Cream and sugar for coffee and tea
Absorbent kitchen paper
Damp j-cloth in a polythene bag
Polythene rubbish bag
Picnic rug or tablecloth
Large umbrella
Matches
Drinking water

Torch

Picnic Tips – Packing

****** If possible, pack *the basket* in the reverse order to that in which the food will be eaten. Put the tablecloth or rug on top so that it can be spread out first (on top it will also provide extra insulation), then directly underneath, the soup Thermos and cups, then the cold meat, etc. This is especially useful for foods that need to be kept chilled. They can be packed in the bottom of the basket with the ice-packs and left undisturbed until needed.

****** Pack *the hors d'œuvres* at the top of the basket. This will make them easily accessible if there is a delay in finding (or deciding upon) a picnic spot. Much better to have your guests arrive at the picnic with just an edge on their appetite rather than ravenous and irritable.

****** Wrap *the cutlery* in brightly coloured napkins so that they're easy to find and not quite so easy to leave behind on the kitchen counter.

****** If you're the slightest bit worried about forgetting *the tin-opener or the corkscrew,* attach it with a rubber band to the bottle or tin itself.

****** Put a small piece of greaseproof or kitchen paper over the tops of the *salt and pepper shakers* and secure with a rubber band to prevent spillage.

****** To save space, pack the *salt and pepper* inside cups or glasses.

****** Pack *the plates* vertically down the sides of the basket. This way they will take up less space and keep containers from sliding against the basket.

****** *Glasses* should be wrapped in napkins or kitchen paper. Even the plastic ones will crack if not protected.

****** Secure the lids on *pâté* or other dishes with Sellotape so they don't slide off in transit and break.

****** Small, shallow wicker baskets are ideal for *packing sandwiches, stuffed vegetables and fruit, cheese,* etc. Lined with a paper napkin, they make an extremely colourful way of presenting food. Their rim also protects the contents and keeps other food in the basket from sliding into them.

****** When packing *the troublesome stuffed egg,* put it into an egg carton instead of on to a plate. To do this, you'll have to cut the hard-boiled eggs in half horizontally and fill that way. They are just as easy to eat done like this but much tidier to pack. Bring along a small spoon to lift the eggs gently out of the carton.

****** To avoid forgetting the *salad dressing,* put it into a small jar and wrap in a square of kitchen paper. Fill the salad bowl with greens, make a well in the centre and fit the jar in. The weight of the greens will keep the jar from falling over and it will be easy to find when ready to toss. Cover the whole bowl with cling film and pack.

Keeping Food Cold

Thermos Flasks

The latest wide-necked Thermos flasks will keep food cold up to six hours. Even ice-cream will stay frozen for at least four hours. Prepare the Thermos by filling with crushed ice, ice-cubes, or ice-cold water. Close and leave for at least fifteen minutes; then empty, dry well with absorbent kitchen paper and fill with the cold food.

The tall, thin Thermos flasks are still the best for cold soups and drinks, being easier to pour than the short, squat kind. Prepare as above.

Crushed Ice

With or without an insulated bag, crushed ice is excellent for keeping food well chilled. Put several ice cubes into a strong polythene bag, squeeze the air out and tie tightly. Then crush the ice with a mallet or rolling pin (but not too forcefully or the bag will split).

Butter and Cream

Put the butter into a small ramekin dish and cover with cling film. Then fill a small round plastic container with crushed ice and bury the ramekin in it (the ice should come half-way up or just to the top of the dish). Do the same with the cream but keep it in its own container.

Vegetables and Fruit

Prepare the crushed ice in a polythene bag as described above, then fill the bag with carrot or celery sticks, radishes or any other vegetable that needs to be kept crisp. For fruit, keep the crushed ice in the polythene bag and use to line the base of a plastic container. Then place the fruit (e.g. peaches, grapes, etc.) on top. If it is a juicy fruit (e.g. strawberries, melon) it must be put into a small dish or container first. This can be half buried in crushed ice or rested on top of the ice, still in its polythene bag.

Cheese

If you want to keep cheese cool but not chilled, line a plastic container with crushed ice (in its polythene bag). Cover with a double layer of absorbent kitchen paper and then rest the cheese (wrapped in cling film) on top. Cover with a lid and pack.

Parsley, Chives, Watercress

Fill a small polythene bag with a handful of crushed ice. Then put chopped chives, parsley or watercress into another small bag and place in the first, resting on the ice. Pack on the top layer of the basket to prevent squashing.

Ice-Packs

These come in a variety of sizes and if frozen completely first will stay cold for about four hours. They should be put into plastic bags before packing so that the condensation doesn't come into contact with the food. If you have enough ice-packs, line the bottom of the basket with them. Then put all the food and drink that needs to be kept chilled on top (lie bottles down flat). Ice-packs can also be moulded to fit a specific container: put them into the right shape before freezing, then put into position round the container.

Ice-Bubbles

These small plastic spheres can be frozen and used in drinks just as you would ice-cubes. Most ironmongers stock them, and as they're usually bright pink they're not difficult to find.

Keeping Food Hot

Thermos Flask

The wide-necked Thermos flask is best for hot foods and thick soups while the tall variety is ideal for other soups and drinks. Prepare the Thermos by filling with hot (but not boiling) water. Close and leave for at least fifteen minutes. Then empty, dry well with absorbent paper (or shake well if this is difficult) and fill with piping hot food. If you have any worries at all about the top not being tight enough then fit a small circle of grease-proof or kitchen paper over the stopper before screwing on. This will prevent leakage.

Aluminium Foil Containers with Lids

These can be found in all shapes and sizes (for really large sizes, try a large kitchen or wholesale catering shop). Fill them with hot food, cover with cardboard lid and seal completely. Then put into the oven and heat until really piping hot. Wrap in foil or put into a strong polythene bag (trap an air bubble in it, then tie tightly) and wrap again in a thick towel, several tea towels or layers of damp newspaper. Or pack in an insulated bag.

Keeping Food Hot and Cold

Insulated Bags and Boxes

These perform the double role of keeping things hot and cold. Some types have various sections so that hot food can be put in one, cold food in another. Without these sections, the insulated bag can only be used to keep food hot *or* cold. Packing them should be done carefully as the food in a half-empty insulated box will slide around when moved. Put wedges of newspaper between the containers to keep them in place. The insulated bags should be packed with the heaviest and sturdiest items at the bottom, working up to the lightest and most perishable. This prevents the food from being squashed and keeps the bag properly balanced.

Extra Insulation

Once the food containers have been filled you can provide them with extra insulation by wrapping them in a thick towel, several tea towels or layers of damp or dry newspaper. The new 'bubble wrap' used to protect stereo equipment and china is also a good insulator. It should be secured with Sellotape after wrapping. The picnic blanket or tablecloth, if placed on top of the basket, will provide further insulation.

2

PÂTÉS, SAVOURY MOUSSES AND HORS D'ŒUVRES

. . . to eat *al fresco* sounds much more delightful than
to picnic – but then it does not possess quite the same
significance; to eat out-of-doors is not enough, otherwise
the every snack of every tramp would constitute a picnic
. . . No, it implies – though this shade of meaning is
contained in no definition of the word to be found in a
dictionary – that one has a home and eats out-of-doors
by choice.

Sir Osbert Sitwell in *Picnics and Pavilions*

It seems particularly appropriate that the Victorians, picnickers
par excellence, referred to hors d'œuvres as 'entrées volantes'.
In other words, 'flying dishes'. Which is what they all too often
are if the picnic basket is travelling by bicycle, British Rail or
pony cart. Though omitted from some picnic menus, they are
in most cases indispensable. Without them, the number of
picnickers who starved while waiting for the fire to light, the
rain to stop or the boats to arrive would increase hourly. As a
rule, there are very few picnics which don't involve some delay
or other (you can count with certainty on at least one traffic
jam). All the more important, then, to have the hors d'œuvres
within easy reach. It won't matter whether they come in the
shape of pâté de foie gras or carrot sticks; it will assuage the
hunger pangs and keep the guests from stampeding to the food
when it does appear.

Pâté, Mousse and Hors D'œuvres Tips

**** To simplify serving, make pâté in individual moulds or small ramekin dishes.

**** Quick pâtés are ideal for last-minute picnics but are more perishable than most and should be eaten the day of making or the day after.

**** Cover pâtés glazed in aspic with foil rather than cling film which will stick to the jelly.

**** Make iced soufflés in small ramekin dishes: they can then be eaten straight from the dish with a spoon or spread on toast like pâté. Cover the dishes with cling film so that they can be stacked one on top of each other in the basket or bag.

**** Pack all hors d'œuvres at the top of the basket, with the exception of heavy pâtés or terrines, so that they are easy to reach.

**** If using a pâté dish or terrine with a lid, secure it first with Sellotape to prevent it falling off and breaking.

Pâtés

PATE MAISON

8oz (225g) streaky unsmoked bacon
8oz (225g) lamb's liver
8oz (225g) belly of pork
1 large onion
3oz (75g) butter
½ pint (275ml) milk (infused with 1 parsley stalk, a few peppercorns, blade of mace)
2 rounded tablespoons flour
½ teaspoon French mustard
1 tablespoon dried or fresh parsley (finely chopped)
salt and pepper to taste
2 bay leaves

27

Pâté dish, terrine or a 1lb (450g) loaf tin

Remove the rind, then stretch the bacon on a chopping board with the back of a knife. Use to line the base and sides of a terrine or loaf tin.

Melt 2oz (50g) of butter in a large saucepan and add the onion, finely chopped. Cut away any tough skin from the belly of pork (if this seems difficult with a knife, use kitchen scissors) and cut into small dice. Chop the lamb's liver into small pieces and put into the saucepan with the pork. Stir until all the pieces are covered with butter, then leave to cook for about 10 minutes.

Pour the milk into a saucepan and add the peppercorns, parsley stalk and blade of mace. Scald, then cover and leave to infuse for 10–15 minutes. Take the meat off the heat and put through a mouli or liquidizer.

Melt the remaining butter (1oz/25g) in a saucepan, take off the heat and stir in the flour. Return to the heat and cook for 1 minute. Then strain the milk and gradually stir in (to prevent lumping, do this off the heat) and bring slowly to the boil. Simmer gently for several minutes until thick. Stir in the mustard, chopped parsley and add salt and pepper to taste. Blend in the minced meat, check the seasoning again, then pour into prepared tin. Press two bay leaves on top and cover with foil or a lid. Put into a roasting tin filled with about 1"/2·5cm water and bake in the centre of a preheated oven (350°F/Gas Mark 4/ 180°C) for 1 hour.

Remove from the roasting tin. Put weights on top and leave to cool. (If you haven't a set of weights, put a plate or tin about the same size on top and use full jars of jam or honey as weights.) Leave in the tin and covered with foil (or with a lid) until needed. To pack for the picnic, wipe the tin well with a damp cloth, cover with a fresh piece of foil and pack (reverse on to a plate just before serving). Or reverse out on to a plate, cover with cling film and pack on the top layer of the basket.

Serves 8

PATE DE CAMPAGNE

8oz (225g) unsmoked streaky
  bacon rashers
8oz (225g) minced veal
8oz (225g) minced pork
8oz (225g) belly of pork
8oz (225g) pig's liver

1 medium onion
2 tablespoons sherry
1 tablespoon chopped parsley
2 teaspoons dried mixed herbs
2 bay leaves
salt and pepper

Pâté dish, terrine or 1½lb (675g) loaf tin

Remove the rind from the bacon rashers, then stretch on a chopping board with the back of a knife. Use to line a terrine or loaf tin.

Cut away any tough skin from the belly of pork and chop into small pieces. Do the same with the liver, removing any large ducts. Chop the onion finely and put into a large mixing bowl with the meats, sherry, parsley, mixed herbs, and a generous sprinkling of salt and pepper. Mix well then press the mixture firmly into the prepared tin and put the two bay leaves on top. Cover tightly with a lid or foil and bake in a bain-marie (a roasting tin half-filled with warm water) in the centre of a pre-heated oven (350°F/Gas Mark 4/180°C) for about 2 hours (or until no pink juices run out of the pâté when pressed with the back of a spoon). Take out of the bain-marie, put weights on top and leave to cool.

This pâté is at its best if left for at least 12 hours before serving so that the flavours have a chance to develop fully. Loosen round the edges with a knife, then reverse out on to a plate. Cover with cling film or foil and pack.

Serves 8

PATE DE PROVENCE

1 medium green pepper
1 medium red pepper
1 medium onion
3oz (75g) butter
2 (7oz/200g) tins of tuna

a good squeeze of lemon juice
2 tablespoons flour
½ pint (275ml) milk (infused with parsley stalk, blade of mace, a few peppercorns)

salt and black pepper to taste

Pâté dish, terrine or 1lb (450g) loaf tin. Grease and line with greaseproof paper, then grease again.

Blanch the two peppers in boiling water, then cut open and remove the white pith and seeds. Chop into small dice. Peel and slice the onion, then chop finely. Melt 2oz (50g) of the butter in a frying pan and sauté the onion and peppers until soft and just about to turn colour.

Put the milk into a small saucepan with the parsley, peppercorns and mace. Scald, then take off the heat and cover. Leave to infuse for at least 15 minutes. In another saucepan, melt the remaining butter and stir in the flour. Cook for 1 minute, then draw off the heat and gradually blend in the strained infused milk. Slowly bring to the boil, then simmer until thick. Season to taste (remembering that the tuna is quite salty) with salt and pepper.

Drain the tuna well, then put into a medium bowl and flake with a fork. Stir in the sauce and add a good squeeze of lemon juice. Check the seasoning and adjust if necessary.

Line the prepared tin with an even layer of half the onion/pepper mixture. Cover with half the tuna, then the remaining onion and peppers and finally the rest of the tuna. Level off the top with the back of a spoon, then cover with a lid or foil and put into a roasting tin half-filled with water. Bake in the centre of a preheated oven (350°F/Gas Mark 4/180°C) for 1 hour.

Remove from the roasting tin, put weights on top and leave to cool. Then loosen round the edges with a knife and reverse out on to a plate. Cover with cling film or foil and pack (or serve straight from the dish).

Serves 8

Quick Pâtés

PATE A LA CREME

4oz (100g) butter
1 clove of garlic
salt
1 large onion
1lb (450g) chicken livers
1 small bay leaf

large pinch of mixed herbs
1 tablespoon brandy or sherry
¼ pint (150ml) double cream
pepper
aspic jelly or melted butter to
   seal

Small pâté dish or earthenware bowl

Melt half the butter in a large frying pan. Crush the garlic with a small amount of salt and add to the pan with the onion, chopped finely. Sauté until soft and transparent.

Chop the livers roughly, removing any large ducts. Add to the onion with the bay leaf and mixed herbs. Cook over moderate heat for about 5 minutes, stirring constantly to prevent sticking, until the liver is cooked on the outside but still slightly pink inside. Add the brandy, mix in well and cook for another minute. Remove the bay leaf and put the mixture through a sieve, mouli or liquidizer. Leave to cool.

Cream the remaining butter in a bowl and blend in the liver purée. Whisk the cream until just thick and fold in. Season to taste with salt and pepper and pour into a pâté dish. Chill well, then cover with a thin layer of aspic jelly or melted butter. To pack: cover with a lid or a loose 'hood' of foil.

Serves 4–6

CHICKEN LIVER PATE WITH ORANGE

1lb (450g) chicken livers
1oz (25g) butter
1 large onion
3oz (75ml) orange juice
grated rind of 1 large orange
1 tablespoon sherry

large pinch of dried herbs
salt and pepper

To decorate:
1 orange
aspic jelly

Small ramekin dishes or earthenware bowl

Chop the livers coarsely, removing any large ducts. Melt the butter in a large frying pan and add the onions, chopped finely. Cook until soft and transparent, then add the livers. Cook quickly over moderate heat until the livers are cooked on the outside but still pink inside (this takes about 5–8 minutes). Put the mixture into a liquidizer, then add the orange juice, orange rind, mixed herbs, sherry, salt and pepper. Blend until smooth. Check the seasoning and adjust if necessary, then pour into the ramekin dishes or a small bowl. Cover with cling film and refrigerate for several hours (or overnight).

To decorate: peel and thinly slice a medium orange and arrange on top of the pâté. Then make up a small amount of aspic jelly according to the manufacturer's instructions. Cool slightly, then coat a thin layer over the oranges and any pâté which is still visible. Chill until set. Cover each dish or the bowl with a loose 'hood' of foil and pack carefully on the top layer of the basket. (You can use cling film but only if there is a gap between the top of the pâté and the rim of the dish, otherwise it will stick to the aspic and spoil the finish.)

Serves 4–6

SMOKED MACKEREL PATE

1lb (450g) smoked mackerel fillets
4oz (100ml) milk
4oz (100g) butter
4½ teaspoons horseradish sauce

a good squeeze of lemon juice
lots of black pepper
6 tablespoons double cream
small bay leaf
a few black peppercorns

Put the mackerel fillets into a large frying pan and cover with the milk. Add a small bay leaf and a few peppercorns, then poach gently until the flesh flakes easily from the bone (this takes 10–15 minutes over moderate heat).

Drain the milk off the fish and carefully remove all the flesh. Put it into the goblet of a liquidizer with the horseradish sauce, a good squeeze of lemon juice and lots of freshly ground black pepper. Melt 3oz (75g) of the butter and add to the ingredients in the liquidizer. Blend again, then pour into individual ramekin dishes or an earthenware bowl. Sprinkle with chopped parsley (fresh or dried). Leave to cool, then melt the remaining butter and coat a thin layer over the top of the pâté.

This pâté is at its best the day of making or the day after.

Serves 4

SPRING PATE

4oz (100g) butter
3 large spring onions
1 large stalk celery
1 (7oz/200g) tin tuna
2 tablespoons mayonnaise

2 ripe tomatoes
2 teaspoons lemon juice
4 tablespoons double cream
salt and freshly ground black pepper

Small pâté dish or earthenware bowl

Wash the spring onions and celery thoroughly, then chop finely. Melt 3½oz (90g) of the butter in a frying pan, and when foaming add the chopped spring onions and celery. Sauté until soft.

Drain the tuna well of oil, then put into a liquidizer. Add the mayonnaise, tomatoes (peeled and chopped roughly), lemon juice, spring onions, celery and the butter remaining in the pan. Blend until smooth, then season to taste with salt and lots of freshly ground black pepper. Add the cream and blend again. Pour into an earthenware dish and leave to cool. Then melt the rest of the butter (adding more if necessary) and use to seal the pâté.

This pâté should be eaten the day it is made or the day after. To pack: cover with a lid, cling film or foil.

Serves 4

AUBERGINE PATE

2 medium aubergines	1 large onion
4oz (100g) butter	large pinch of mixed herbs
2½ tablespoons olive or vegetable oil	salt and black pepper

Small pâté dish or earthenware bowl

Wash the aubergines and dry well. Slice the tops off, then cut in half lengthwise. Score the surfaces with a knife and sprinkle liberally with salt. Put on a plate and leave for at least 15 minutes. Then wipe dry with absorbent kitchen paper.

Melt half the butter in a large frying pan and heat with the vegetable oil. Chop the onion finely and sauté until soft. Cut the aubergine into medium dice and add to the pan. Cook for 30–45 minutes, shaking the pan or stirring from time to time, until the vegetables are very soft and starting to brown. Add another ounce (25g) of butter to the pan and, when melted, pour the contents of the pan into a liquidizer. Add salt and pepper, a pinch of mixed herbs and blend until smooth. Pour into a pâté dish or earthenware bowl and chill. When quite cold, melt the remaining butter (1oz/25g) and pour over the pâté to seal. (This pâté will keep for 4–5 days.)

Serves 4–6

CAULIFLOWER CHEESE PATE

An old favourite turns up in yet another guise.

½ pint (275ml) milk (infused with bay leaf, parsley stalk, a few peppercorns)
1 large cauliflower
1oz (25g) butter

2 rounded tablespoons flour
¼ teaspoon French mustard
3oz (75g) mature cheddar cheese
salt and white pepper to taste
dried breadcrumbs

Grease a small pâté dish or earthenware bowl. Cut a circle of greaseproof paper to fit the bottom, press in firmly, then grease again. Toss in a small amount of breadcrumbs and swirl round the bottom and sides of the dish until well coated in the crumbs.

Put the milk in a saucepan with the bay leaf, parsley stalk and a few peppercorns. Heat to scalding point, then take off the heat, cover and leave to infuse for at least 15 minutes.

Cook the cauliflower in a small amount of water until very soft. Drain thoroughly, then put back into the saucepan and pound until smooth with a potato masher. Heat gently for about 5 minutes, shaking the pan from time to time, to dry the cauliflower out further. Then put to one side.

Melt the butter in a saucepan, stir in the flour and cook for 1 minute. Take off the heat and gradually blend in the strained infused milk. Cook over moderate heat until the mixture thickens and boils. Then add the mustard and seasonings and continue cooking until quite thick. Add the cheese and stir until completely blended (being careful not to let it boil again).

Stir the mashed cauliflower into the sauce, check the seasoning, then pour into prepared dish. Cover with foil and bake in a bain-marie (filled with about an inch (2·5cm) of warm water) in a preheated oven (350°F/Gas Mark 4/180°C) for an hour. Take out, put a heavy weight on top and leave to cool. Cover with a clean piece of foil and pack. Either serve straight from the dish or loosen round the sides with a knife and reverse out on to a plate. (It is also very attractive if made in small ramekins and then reversed out on to individual plates.)

Serves 6–8

Soufflés and Mousses

COLD ASPARAGUS SOUFFLE

1 (12oz/340g) tin of asparagus
½oz (15g) gelatine
5 tablespoons mayonnaise
½ chicken stock cube

8oz (225ml) boiling water
2 large egg whites
¼ pint (150ml) double cream
salt and pepper

6–8 ramekin dishes or 1 small soufflé dish

Drain the asparagus and reserve the juice. Put 4 tablespoons of the juice into a small cup and sprinkle the gelatine on top. Leave it to soak for 5 minutes, then stand the cup in hot water until the gelatine has completely dissolved. Put to one side to cool slightly. Dissolve the chicken stock cube in the boiling water, then leave to cool.

Put the asparagus into a liquidizer with the mayonnaise, salt and pepper and blend on low speed until smooth. Pour in the slightly cooled chicken stock and blend again. Take the centre top cap off the liquidizer and, at low speed, pour in the gelatine in a steady stream. When well blended, pour into a bowl and put into the refrigerator to cool (or stir over a bowl of ice-cubes until the mixture starts to thicken).

When the mixture is just starting to set (about the consistency of egg white), whisk the cream until thick and fold in lightly.

Then whisk the egg whites until stiff and fold in. Pour into a soufflé dish or small ramekins. Chill until set, then cover with foil or cling film and pack. Serve with brown bread and butter.

Serves 6

ICED SALMON SOUFFLE

¼ pint (150ml) milk (infused with slice of onion, small bay leaf, parsley stalk and a few peppercorns)
1½ level teaspoons gelatine
1 tablespoon lemon juice
1 tablespoon water
½oz (15g) butter

1 level tablespoon flour
2 teaspoons dried parsley
1 (7½oz/211g) tin red or pink salmon
4 tablespoons mayonnaise
salt and pepper to taste
2 large egg whites
3oz (75ml) double cream

Ramekin dishes or small soufflé dish

Put the milk in a small saucepan with the parsley, onion, bay leaf and peppercorns. Scald, then cover, take off the heat and leave to infuse for at least 5 minutes. Pour the water and lemon juice into a cup and sprinkle the gelatine on top. Leave to soak for 5 minutes, then put the cup over or in hot water until the gelatine has dissolved completely. Set aside and cool to luke-warm.

In another saucepan, melt the butter. Add the flour and mix in well. Then take off the heat and gradually blend in the strained infused milk. Stir over moderate heat until the mixture thickens and boils. Reduce the heat and simmer until the sauce is quite thick. Season well with salt and pepper and stir in the parsley. Take off the heat and whisk well for a minute or two, then put to one side.

Drain the salmon well and remove all bones and skin. Put into a mixing bowl and flake with a fork. Then blend in the mayonnaise and the béchamel sauce. Pour the gelatine in a steady stream into the bowl and mix until well blended. Whisk the cream until just thick and fold in. Whisk the egg whites until stiff and fold in lightly. Pour into individual ramekins or a small soufflé dish. Chill until set, then cover with cling film and pack. Serve with crusty rolls and butter.

Serves 6

CUCUMBER AND HAM MOUSSE

1 small cucumber
½oz (15g) butter
1 very small onion
2 slices of cooked ham
2 teaspoons lemon juice
1 tablespoon water
1½ teaspoons gelatine

7oz (200ml) well-seasoned chicken stock (or ½ chicken stock cube dissolved in 7oz/ 200ml boiling water)
4oz (100g) cream cheese
1½ tablespoons mayonnaise
salt and white pepper to taste

3oz (75ml) double cream

6–8 ramekin dishes

Peel the cucumber and slice thinly. Put on a plate, sprinkle generously with salt and leave for 30 minutes. Then pour the liquid off and dry the cucumber with absorbent kitchen paper. Cut into small dice.

Chop the onion and ham finely and sauté in the butter until the onion is soft and just turning colour. Remove from the pan and leave to cool. Put the lemon juice and water into a small cup and sprinkle the gelatine on top. Leave to soak for 5 minutes, then put the cup over or in hot water until the gelatine has completely dissolved. Cool to lukewarm.

Put the diced cucumber into a liquidizer with the chicken stock and blend until smooth. Add the ham and onion mixture and blend again. Gradually add the cream cheese and mayonnaise. With the blender on low speed, pour in the cooled gelatine in a steady stream. Give a final whiz on high speed, then pour into a mixing bowl. Season to taste with salt and pepper, then stand the bowl in a pan of ice-cubes and stir until it begins to thicken (or put into the refrigerator and leave until it starts to set, stirring occasionally).

Whisk the cream until just thick and when the cucumber mixture starts to thicken, fold in lightly. Check the seasoning and adjust if necessary, then pour into the ramekin dishes. Chill until set, then cover with cling film and pack (decorate each dish with a thin slice of cucumber before covering, if you wish).

Serves 6–8

EGG MOUSSE DIJONNAIS

¼ pint (150ml) milk (infused with small bay leaf, a few peppercorns, parsley stalk, blade of mace)	1 rounded tablespoon flour salt and pepper to taste 1½ teaspoons Dijon mustard 4 large hard-boiled eggs
1½ level teaspoons gelatine	3 tablespoons mayonnaise
2 tablespoons water	3oz (75ml) double cream
1½oz (40g) butter	2 large egg whites
chopped parsley to decorate	

6–8 ramekin dishes

Put the milk in a small saucepan with the bay leaf, peppercorns, parsley stalk and blade of mace. Scald, then take off the heat, cover and leave to infuse for at least 15 minutes. Put 2 tablespoons of cold water into a cup and sprinkle the gelatine on top. Leave to soak for 5 minutes then put the cup over or in hot water until the gelatine has completely dissolved. Cool to lukewarm.

Melt ½oz (15g) of butter in a saucepan and stir in the flour. Take off the heat and gradually blend in the strained, infused milk. Cook over gentle heat until the mixture thickens and boils. Season to taste with salt and white pepper, then mix in the mustard, and remaining butter. Pour in the lukewarm gelatine in a steady stream and whisk in well. Put to one side.

Chop the eggs very finely and put into a large mixing bowl.

Blend in the mayonnaise and then the sauce. Check the season-ing and adjust if necessary. Whisk the cream until just thick and fold in with the egg whites, whisked until stiff. Pour into ramekin dishes and chill until set. Decorate with chopped parsley, cover with cling film and pack. This mousse is rather rich and is best eaten as a pâté, with brown bread and butter.

Serves 8

Quick hors d'œuvres

CRUDITES AND DIPS

This is an easy starter and one which takes the edge off the appetite without satisfying it completely. The vegetables can be packed in a polythene bag filled with a small amount of crushed ice and the dips can be put into small ramekin dishes or plastic containers, covered with foil or cling film.

Wash and drain any of the following and chop into julienne strips or bite-size pieces, then use with the dips given below:

Cauliflower	Green or Red Peppers
Carrots	Lettuce Hearts
Celery	Spring Onions
Cucumber	Radishes
Courgettes	Small Tomatoes

SOUR CREAM AND ONION DIP

1 packet of dried onion soup
2 (5oz/150ml) cartons sour
  cream

Put the sour cream into a mixing bowl and whisk until smooth. Then gradually whisk in the dried onion soup to taste (remembering that the flavour will become more pronounced if it is made some time in advance). Finish off with a sprinkling of the dried soup on top and chill until needed.

PINEAPPLE CHEESE DIP

1 small tin (8oz/225g) pineapple chunks

1 (8oz/225g) carton of cottage cheese

1 (3oz/75g) packet of cream cheese

sugar to taste

Drain the pineapple chunks and put the juice to one side. Reserve several chunks for decoration and put the rest into a liquidizer. Add the cottage cheese, cream cheese (cut into small pieces) and blend until smooth. Add sugar to taste and just enough of the pineapple juice to give it a creamy (but not watery) consistency. Chill for several hours before using.

BACON DIP

6 rashers of streaky bacon
2 teaspoons bacon fat
1½ tablespoons mayonnaise
6oz (175g) cream cheese

6–8 tablespoons milk
1½ teaspoons dried onions
chopped parsley (fresh or dried)

salt and pepper to taste

Put all the ingredients into a liquidizer and blend until smooth, adding more milk if too thick. Put into a bowl, cover with cling film and chill until needed. Check the consistency again before packing: it may need to be thinned with several tablespoons of milk. Sprinkle with chopped parsley.

ROQUEFORT DIP

4oz (100g) Roquefort or any blue cheese

3oz (75g) cream cheese
¼ pint (150ml) single cream

Put all ingredients into a liquidizer and blend until smooth, adding a small amount of milk if too thick. Transfer to a bowl or plastic container, cover with a lid or cling film and refrigerate until needed.

PATE FILLED CROISSANTS

1 small package (7½oz/212g) frozen puff pastry

6oz (175g) smooth pâté*
beaten egg to glaze

Grease a large baking tray.
Preheat oven to 400°F/Gas Mark 6/200°C.

Let the pastry thaw until just pliable enough to handle (but don't let it get soft). Divide the dough in two and roll each half out into a thin circle on a lightly floured counter. With the back of a knife mark each circle into six triangles and then cut out. Roll each triangle again so that it is very thin, then spread with pâté (keeping it about ⅛"/·25cm from the edges). Roll up from the longest side to the shortest, sealing the tip of the triangle with a small amount of cold water. Twist into a crescent shape, then place on the baking tray and brush lightly with beaten egg. Make the others in the same way, then bake in the centre of a preheated oven for about 25 minutes or until golden brown. Cool on a wire rack and pack in a plastic bag or tin.

Makes 12 croissants

* If you haven't any home-made pâté, the tinned French brands are very good for this, as is the range of Marks & Spencer pâtés.

POTTED CHEESE AND WALNUTS

2oz (50g) butter
4oz (100g) cheddar cheese, grated

1½oz (40g) chopped walnuts
3oz (75ml) single cream or rich milk

1 teaspoon port, wine or cherry

Large ramekin dish or small earthenware bowl

Put the butter and cheese into a bowl and fit into a saucepan filled with a small amount of gently simmering water. Leave until both are completely melted, then take off the heat and leave to cool slightly. Whisk until smooth, then gradually whisk in the cream (or milk) and the wine. Fold in two-thirds of the chopped walnuts and pour into a large ramekin dish. Sprinkle the remaining walnuts on top. Chill for several hours then cover with cling film or foil and pack. Serve with wholemeal bread, melba toast or crostini.

Serves 4

BOURSIN BISCUITS

1 packet of high-baked water biscuits
1 (5oz/150g) packet Boursin cheese

2–3 teaspoons cream or top of the milk
1–2 tablespoons redcurrant jelly

Soften the Boursin cheese in a bowl with a fork. Add just enough cream to make it smooth (without being moist). Then spread a thick layer over each water biscuit and put a small circle of redcurrant jelly in the centre. You can make as many or as few of these as you like; for a smaller number divide the quantities given above by half. Pack the biscuits in a tin. (They must be made the day of the picnic.)

COCKTAIL SAUSAGES AND MUSTARD

1–2 small packages cocktail
  sausages

1 small jar French mustard
  olive oil or cream
  toothpicks

Cook the sausages according to the instructions on the packet, then drain. Put straight into an aluminium-foil container with a lid and pack in an insulated bag or leave to cool, then put into a plastic container. Dilute the French mustard slightly with olive oil or cream, then put into a small ramekin dish and cover with cling film. When ready to serve, pass around the sausages with the toothpicks and mustard.

MELON WITH PROSCIUTTO HAM

1 small melon
thin slices of Prosciutto or
  cooked ham

a good squeeze of lemon
  juice
toothpicks

Cut the melon into good-sized chunks and the ham into short, thin strips. Wrap each piece of melon in a strip of ham and secure with a toothpick. Stand up in a plastic container and sprinkle with lemon juice. Cover with a lid and chill until needed.

Recipes for the following can be found in other parts of the book: Terrine de canard (p. 243), Chinese meatballs (p. 127), Mini Pizzas (p. 112), Stuffed Celery (p. 94), Pâté and Bacon Crostini (p. 80).

3
SOUPS

Beautiful Soup! Who cares for fish,
Game, or any other dish?
Who would not give all else for two p
ennyworth only of beautiful Soup?

The Mock Turtle in *Alice's Adventures in Wonderland*

It only takes one wet picnic to make you realize that *nothing* is more important than hot soup. It warms the bones and revitalizes the spirit in a way that few other things do. And it's cheaper than brandy and lighter to carry than a duffle coat! It's extremely versatile and many recipes for hot soup can be converted to icy cold ones for summer.

For tips on packing hot and chilled soups, see the introductory section on Packing (pp. 21–4).

Hot Soups

CREAMY VEGETABLE SOUP

1 pint (575ml) milk (infused with ½ small onion, blade of mace, a few peppercorns, parsley stalk)
4oz (100g) carrots
1 small potato
4oz (100g) french beans
4oz (100g) peas
2 large stalks celery

1¼ pints (700ml) well-seasoned chicken stock (or 1½ chicken stock cubes dissolved in 1¼ pints boiling water)
2oz (50g) butter
4 level tablespoons flour
1 tablespoon chopped parsley (fresh or dried)
salt and pepper to taste

45

Slice the onion thinly, then put into a saucepan with the milk, blade of mace, peppercorns and parsley stalk. Scald, then take off the heat. Cover and leave to infuse for at least 15 minutes.

Peel the carrots and the potato, then chop into small dice. Wash and drain the beans and celery. Cut into thin strips, about ½″ (1cm) long. Dissolve the chicken stock cubes in the boiling water (or use fresh stock), put into a large saucepan and bring to the boil. Add the vegetables, bring back to the boil, then cover and reduce the heat. Simmer gently until the vegetables are tender. Drain the juice into a jug and put the vegetables into a bowl.

Melt the butter in a large saucepan, stir in the flour and cook for 1 minute. Take off the heat and gradually blend in the strained infused milk. Return to the heat and stir until the mixture thickens and boils. Continue cooking over gentle heat (stirring constantly) and gradually add the stock from the vegetables. When it has all been blended in, add the vegetables and parsley, then season to taste with salt and pepper. Slowly reheat until just about to boil. Check the seasoning, then pour into a warmed Thermos or refrigerate until needed, then reheat.

Serves 6–8

CELERY AND CHEESE SOUP

2oz (50g) butter
1 medium onion
1 large head of celery
1½ pints (850ml) chicken stock
4 level tablespoons flour
3oz (75g) grated cheddar

cheese (or cheddar and parmesan mixed)
½ pint (275ml) milk
pinch of dry mustard
pinch of grated nutmeg
salt and pepper to taste

Melt half the butter in a large saucepan and, when foaming, add the onion, finely chopped. Cook for about 5 minutes, then add the celery, cut into small dice. Cover and cook for a further 5 minutes. Then add the chicken stock and cook over moderate heat for 20 minutes.

In another saucepan, melt the remaining butter, add the flour and cook for 1 minute. Then stir in the milk, mix well and slowly bring to the boil. Simmer gently until thick, then stir in the grated cheddar, dry mustard, and nutmeg. Season to taste with salt and pepper.

When the celery is tender, pour off the juices in the pan and gradually blend them into the white sauce. Put the celery through a mouli, sieve or liquidizer, then add to the soup. Check the seasoning and slowly reheat, being careful not to let the mixture boil. Pour straight into a warmed Thermos or refrigerate until needed, then reheat.

Serves 6–8

CORN CHOWDER

4oz (100g) bacon rashers
 (½ gammon, ½ streaky)
1oz (25g) butter
3 large stalks celery
1 large onion
1 small green pepper
2 level tablespoons flour
½lb (225g) potatoes

1½ chicken stock cubes
1 pint (575ml) milk
1 (12oz/350g) tin sweetcorn
 kernels
small bay leaf
salt and black pepper
chopped parsley (fresh or
 dried)

Remove the rind and chop the bacon into small pieces. Then chop the onion and celery finely. Melt the butter in a large saucepan and toss the bacon dice in it. Cook until almost crisp (stirring occasionally to prevent sticking), then add the chopped onion and celery and continue cooking until the onion is soft and transparent.

Slice the top off the green pepper, remove the white pith and seeds, then chop into small pieces. Peel and chop the potatoes into chunks (not too small or they will disintegrate during cooking). When the onion is just about to turn colour, stir in the flour and cook for a minute or two. Dissolve the chicken stock cubes in 1 pint (575ml) boiling water and stir in gradually. When well blended, add the potatoes, green pepper, bay leaf and a good sprinkling of salt and black pepper. Bring back to the boil, then reduce the heat and simmer gently for about 20 minutes or until the vegetables are tender. Add the milk and sweetcorn (drain well first) and heat very gently (being careful not to let it boil) for a further 30 minutes, stirring from time to time. Sprinkle with chopped parsley, check the seasoning and remove the bay leaf. Pour into a warmed Thermos or refrigerate until needed, then reheat.

Serves 4–6

MINESTRONE

Making minestrone takes a little more time than most soups but is always worth the effort. This recipe makes quite a large quantity so that half can be taken on the picnic and the other half frozen for the next one.

2oz (50g) butter
1 gammon rasher (or 2 streaky bacon rashers)
4 large carrots
1 large onion
2 large celery stalks
½ small cabbage
2 leeks
8oz (225g) french beans

2½ pints (1·5 litres) chicken stock
1 (14oz/398g) tin of tomatoes
3 tablespoons tomato purée
2 teaspoons sugar
1 bouquet garni
1 small bay leaf
salt and black pepper
4 tablespoons Parmesan cheese

Wash and peel the carrots and cut into medium dice. Chop the onion and celery finely, then cut the gammon rasher into small pieces. Melt the butter in a large saucepan and add the chopped gammon, onion, carrots and celery. Stir until they are well coated in the butter, then cook over gentle heat until the onion is soft and transparent. Shake the pan occasionally to keep the vegetables from sticking.

Wash and shred the cabbage and leeks, then add to the saucepan with the french beans (cut into 1″/2·5cm lengths), chicken stock, tomato purée, sugar, tomatoes, bay leaf and bouquet garni. Bring to the boil, then reduce the heat and simmer gently for 1½–2 hours. Season to taste with salt and freshly ground black pepper. Add the Parmesan cheese and remove the bay leaf and bouquet garni. Ladle into a warmed wide-necked Thermos and refrigerate or freeze the remainder until needed, then reheat.

Serves 14–16

Hot or Cold Soups

CREAM OF WATERCRESS SOUP

2 large bunches of watercress	¾ pint (425ml) milk
1 medium onion	¼ pint (150ml) single cream
1oz (25g) butter	2 egg yolks
2 level tablespoons flour	salt and black pepper
¾ pint (425ml) well-seasoned chicken stock	pinch of nutmeg

Wash the watercress thoroughly and chop roughly. Melt the butter in a large saucepan and add the onion, chopped finely. Stir until thoroughly coated in the butter and cook until soft and transparent (but not coloured). Stir in the flour and cook for 1 minute. Then add the watercress, cover and 'sweat' for several minutes. Pour on the chicken stock and simmer gently for 15 minutes. Put through a mouli or blender, then return to the pan. Add the milk and gradually bring back to the boil. Season to taste with salt and pepper, then take off the heat.

Mix the egg yolks and cream together in a small basin. Gradually add several spoonfuls of the hot soup to it, then pour back into the saucepan. Slowly reheat, being careful not to let it boil. If serving hot, pour into a warmed Thermos and pack. For cold soup, refrigerate until needed, then pour into a chilled Thermos.

Serves 4–6

POTAGE VERT

1 medium onion
1oz (25g) butter
2 level tablespoons flour
1 pint (575ml) strong chicken stock (or 1½ chicken stock cubes dissolved in 1 pint boiling water)

1 bunch of watercress
handful of spinach
8 large lettuce leaves
1½ pints (850ml) milk
salt and pepper
large pinch of ground nutmeg

Chop the onion finely and sauté in the butter until soft and transparent. Stir in the flour and cook for 1 minute. Blend in the chicken stock gradually and bring to the boil.

Wash the watercress, spinach and lettuce thoroughly, then drain. Shred roughly and add to the boiling stock. Cover, reduce the heat and simmer gently for about 20 minutes. Put through a sieve, mouli or liquidizer, then return to the pan. Add salt and pepper to taste and a large pinch of nutmeg. Stir in the milk and gently reheat until just about to boil. Check the seasoning and adjust if necessary. Pour straight into a warmed Thermos or chill for several hours, then pour into an icy cold one.

Whether served hot or cold, this soup is always improved with a dollop of cream, added just before serving.

Serves 6

LEEK AND POTATO SOUP

3 large leeks
8 good-sized spring onions
2oz (50g) butter
¾lb (350g) potatoes (3 medium)
chopped chives (fresh or dried)

1½ pints (850ml) chicken stock
½ pint (275ml) milk
¼ pint (150ml) single cream*
salt and pepper to taste

* An equal quantity of rich milk can be used instead, if you prefer.

Cut the leeks in half lengthwise, wash thoroughly and shred. Do the same with the spring onions. Then put the butter in a large saucepan and, when foaming, add the chopped leeks and spring onions. Cook for 5–10 minutes or until the onion is soft, stirring occasionally.

Peel and chop the potatoes into small dice and add to the pan with the stock. Cover and cook over moderate heat for 20 minutes or until the potatoes are cooked through. Put through a mouli, sieve, or liquidizer, then return to the pan. Stir in the milk, cream, salt and pepper and slowly reheat to just below boiling point. Check the seasoning and adjust if necessary, then sprinkle with chopped chives. Pour into a warmed Thermos or chill for several hours and pour into an icy cold one. (If serving cold, you may want to dilute it slightly with cream or milk.)

Serves 4–6

FRENCH PEA SOUP

1oz (25g) butter
1 medium onion
2 level tablespoons flour
8 large lettuce leaves
8oz (225g) peas (fresh or frozen)

1 pint (575ml) strong chicken stock
1 pint (575ml) milk
salt and pepper
sprig of fresh mint (or a good pinch of dried mint)

Melt the butter in a large saucepan. Chop the onion and sauté until soft but not coloured. Then stir in the flour and cook for 1 minute.

Wash the lettuce well and dry in a clean tea towel or absorbent kitchen paper. Shred and add to the ingredients in the saucepan. Add the peas and stock. Bring to the boil, then reduce the heat and simmer gently for 10 minutes. Put the soup through a sieve or liquidizer, then return to the pan. Add the milk, mint and season to taste with salt and pepper. Cook, stirring from time to time, over gentle heat for a further 20–30 minutes. Then remove the sprig of mint and pour into a warmed Thermos flask.

If serving cold, chill for several hours, then dilute (if necessary) with milk or cream. Remove the sprig of mint and pour into an icy cold Thermos.

Serves 4–6

For an early twentieth-century version of pea soup, see Osborne Soup in *The Go-Between Picnic* (p. 211).

Quick Soups

TOMATO AND ORANGE SOUP

1 medium onion	1 (14oz/398g) tin tomatoes
2oz (50g) butter	12oz (350ml) orange juice
2 level tablespoons flour	2 teaspoons sugar
1 (19oz/540ml) tin tomato juice	½ teaspoon dried basil or thyme
	salt and black pepper

Chop the onion finely and sauté in the butter until soft but not coloured. Stir in the flour and cook for 1 minute. Then add the tomatoes, tomato and orange juices, sugar, basil (or thyme) and slowly bring to the boil. Then reduce the heat and simmer gently for about 5 minutes. Put the soup through a sieve, mouli or liquidizer, then return to the pan. Season to taste with salt and black pepper. Pour straight into a warmed Thermos or chill for several hours, then pour into an icy cold one. (If serving cold, you might like to dilute it slightly with milk or cream.)

Serves 6

SPINACH SOUP

---

1 (8oz/225g) packet frozen
  chopped spinach
1oz (25g) butter
1 medium onion
2 level tablespoons flour

1½ chicken stock cubes
1 pint (575ml) boiling water
½ pint (275ml) milk
large pinch ground nutmeg
salt and black pepper

Put the frozen spinach in a saucepan over low heat. Cover and leave until completely thawed and quite dry (shake the pan occasionally to prevent sticking).

In another saucepan, melt the butter and add the onion, chopped finely. Sauté until the onion is soft and transparent, then stir in the flour. Cook for 1 minute. Dissolve the stock cubes in the boiling water and gradually add (off the heat) to the pan. Return to the heat and bring slowly to the boil. Add the spinach, a large pinch of nutmeg, salt and pepper. Put the soup through a sieve, Mouli or liquidizer until smooth. Pour back into the pan and add the milk. Gradually reheat until just about to boil. Check the seasoning, then pour into a warmed Thermos and pack. Or chill thoroughly, dilute slightly with milk or cream and put into a cold Thermos.

Serves 4

GAZPACHO

---

1 large (1lb 12oz/793g) tin
  tomatoes
1 (19oz/540ml) tin tomato
  juice
2 teaspoons sugar
large pinch dried thyme
1 teaspoon chopped parsley
  (fresh or dried)
3 tablespoons olive oil
2 tablespoons wine vinegar

3 large slices white bread
1 large cucumber
1 green pepper
2 large stalks celery
8 spring onions (or 1 small
  onion)
1 pint (575ml) chicken stock
1 clove garlic
salt and lots of black pepper
croûtons
  chopped chives

Put the tomatoes and tomato juice into a large bowl and stir in the sugar, thyme, parsley, olive oil and vinegar. Remove the crusts, then crumble the bread into the bowl and blend in. Chop the cucumber (no need to peel it) into small dice and put half into the mixing bowl and half to one side. Do the same with the green pepper, celery and spring onions.

Stir the chicken stock into the tomato mixture. Crush the garlic with the tip of a knife in a small amount of salt, and add. Then pour the soup, by thirds, into the liquidizer and blend for a very short time (several seconds only), just long enough to break down the vegetables slightly. Pour into a large bowl, stir in the remaining vegetables and season to taste with salt and freshly ground black pepper. Chill for several hours, then pour into a cold Thermos. Fill a small polythene bag with croûtons, another with chopped chives, and add these to the soup just before serving (these aren't absolutely necessary but do make a delicious finishing touch).

Serves 8–10

CREAM OF MUSHROOM SOUP

1lb (450g) button mushrooms	1 pint (575ml) boiling water
1oz (25g) butter	½ pint (275ml) milk
1 small onion	¼ pint (150ml) single cream
2 rounded tablespoons flour	1 tablespoon sherry (optional)
1¼ chicken stock cubes	salt and white pepper

Wash the mushrooms and wipe dry with absorbent kitchen paper. Then chop (including the stalks) into very small dice.

Melt the butter in a large saucepan and add the onion, chopped finely. Cook until soft and transparent, then add the mushrooms. Cook for a further 10–15 minutes until the mushrooms are soft and have darkened in colour. Add the flour and cook for 1 minute. Dissolve the stock cubes in the boiling water and gradually add to the pan (off the heat). Slowly bring to the boil, stirring occasionally. Add the milk and a good sprinkling of salt and pepper. Simmer for a further 15–20 minutes, then add the cream and the sherry. Heat gently until very hot (being careful not to let it boil), then check the seasoning and pour into a warmed Thermos. (Or chill until needed, then reheat.)

Serves 4

Recipes for the following can be found in other parts of the book: Osborne Soup (p. 211), Chicken Gumbo Soup (p. 249).

4

BREADS

A loaf of bread is what we chiefly need . . .

Walrus from *Through the Looking Glass*

The difference between store-bought and home-made bread is so considerable that it is well worth the time and effort to bake your own. Bread-making doesn't need to be time-consuming or complicated. The recipes given in this chapter are among the easiest to master and many use the new method of yeast cookery in which ascorbic acid is used to speed up the rising. This means that you can make a loaf of bread in almost half the time it used to take. Ideal for picnics!

Bread-Making Tips

***** Always make sure that the mixing bowls, tins, etc., are warmed before using, as any coldness will slow down the rising process.

***** If you haven't a warm place to leave the dough while rising, then put it in a covered bowl on the top shelf of the oven. Turn the oven on to its lowest temperature and leave the oven door open. Check from time to time to make sure that the air inside is just slightly warm and not hot.

***** Use ascorbic acid tablets with fresh yeast for the fastest results; the slower rising action of dried yeast will impede the action of the ascorbic acid slightly.

***** *For a soft crust,* cover the bread while cooling with a clean tea towel. *For a crisp crust,* take the bread out of the tin when it is done and return to the oven for 5–10 minutes. *For a crisp crust and soft sides,* cool uncovered. *For a rich, glossy crust,* brush the top of the loaf with melted butter when it comes out of the oven.

***** Store and pack bread in a polythene bag; it will stay much fresher than if kept in a tin.

***** For quick reference: a 2lb (1kg) loaf tin measures 9″ (23cm) in length; a 1lb (450g) tin, 6½″ (16·5cm) or 7″ (17·5cm).

WHITE BREAD (Quick Method)

Yeast Liquid:
½oz (15g) fresh yeast
1 (1oz/25g) ascorbic acid
  tablet
15oz (425ml) lukewarm water

Dough:
1½lb (675g) strong white flour
1 tablespoon salt
2 teaspoons sugar
½oz (15g) lard

Grease one 2lb (1kg) tin, two 1lb (450g) tins or a 1lb loaf tin and baking tray.

Crush the ascorbic acid tablet to a fine powder and mix with the yeast in the lukewarm water. Stir until the yeast has completely dissolved.

Put the flour in a large mixing bowl and mix in the sugar and salt, then rub in the lard. Make a well in the centre and pour in the yeast liquid. Mix with a large wooden spoon or fork until the dough leaves the sides of the bowl clean and forms a ball in the centre. Turn out on to a lightly floured counter and knead until it becomes smooth and elastic (this takes 5–10 minutes). Put back into the bowl and cover with a lightly greased polythene bag. Leave to rest for 5 minutes.

Turn the dough out on to a counter and pummel with knuckles to get rid of any large air bubbles. Then flatten out into a large rectangle (its width should equal the length of the tin; its length should be three times the width of the tin). Fold into three, tuck the ends under and put into greased tin. Press the dough well into the corners. *If making two 1lb loaves:* divide the dough in half, flatten into two oblongs (see above for size), fold in three, tuck the ends under and place in greased tins. *To make a 1lb loaf and rolls:* divide the dough in half and use one part to make a loaf, as described above. Divide the remaining dough into 2oz (50g) portions and shape into rolls. *To make cloverleaf rolls:* divide each portion into three equal parts and roll between your hands to make smooth balls. Place these close together in a triangular formation on a greased baking tray. *To make picnic rolls:* knead each portion of dough into a round shape and place on greased baking tray. *To make finger rolls:* flatten each portion out into a rectangle, fold into three (or roll up, swiss-roll style), tuck the ends under or seal with the side of your hand and place on greased tray. Place close together for soft-sided rolls or well apart for crusty ones.

Put the tins inside a greased polythene bag and leave in a warm place until the dough has doubled in size (it should spring back when touched lightly with a floured finger). Then remove the bag, brush with milk or beaten egg and bake in the centre (or second shelf from the top for rolls) of a preheated oven (450°F/Gas Mark 8/200°C) for 30 minutes (20 minutes for rolls). To test if the bread is done: rap the base with knuckles: if it sounds hollow, it's ready to come out. Loosen round the edges of the tin with a knife, then reverse out on to a wire rack. Turn right side up and leave to cool.

Makes 1 large or 2 small loaves or 1 small loaf and approximately 8 rolls

QUICK WHOLEWHEAT LOAF AND ROLLS

Yeast Liquid:
1 level tablespoon dried yeast
1 teaspoon brown sugar
1 (1oz/25g) ascorbic acid
   tablet
5oz (150ml) hand-hot water

Dough:
1½lb (675g) wholewheat flour
1 level tablespoon salt
1oz (25g) butter/margarine
3 level tablespoons malt extract
5oz (150ml) water
5oz (150ml) milk

Grease a 1lb (450g) loaf tin and a baking tray.

Crush the ascorbic acid tablet to a fine powder and mix with the dried yeast and sugar in the hand-hot water. Leave in a warm place until frothy (this takes about 15 minutes).

Put the flour in a large mixing bowl and mix in the salt, then rub in the fat. Put the malt extract in a saucepan with the milk and water. Stir over low heat until completely blended, then cool to lukewarm. Make a well in the centre of the dry ingredients and pour in the yeast liquid with the malt mixture. Stir with a large wooden spoon or fork until the dough leaves the sides of the bowl clean. Then turn out on to a lightly floured counter. Knead until the dough is smooth and elastic, then put back into the bowl. Cover with a greased polythene bag and leave to rest for 5 minutes.

Turn the dough out on to a lightly floured counter and pummel with knuckles to knock out large air bubbles. Then knead back into shape. Divide the dough in half. Take one part and flatten it into an oblong (its width should equal the length of the tin; its length should be three times the width of the tin). Then roll up (swiss-roll style) or fold into three, tuck the ends under and place in greased tin. Divide the remaining dough into 2oz (50g) portions and shape into rolls (for roll shapes, see White Bread recipe). Put the rolls well apart on a greased baking tray. Put the tin and tray inside a greased polythene bag and leave in a warm place until the dough has doubled in size. Then remove the bag and brush the loaf and rolls lightly with salted water. Bake the loaf in the centre of the oven (preheated to 425°F/Gas Mark 7/ 220°C) for about 30 minutes and the rolls on the second shelf from the top for about 20 minutes. Cool on a wire rack.

Makes 1 small loaf and approximately 8 rolls

ENRICHED BREAD (Quick Method)

Yeast Liquid:
1oz (25g) fresh yeast
1 (1oz/25g) ascorbic acid tablet
8oz (225ml) lukewarm milk

Dough:
1lb (450g) strong white flour
1 teaspoon sugar
1 teaspoon salt
2oz (50g) butter/margarine
1 standard egg, lightly beaten

Grease a baking tray or an 8" (20cm) sandwich tin (at least 1"/ 2·5cm deep).

Crush the ascorbic acid tablet to a fine powder and dissolve in the lukewarm milk with the yeast.

Put the flour in a large mixing bowl and mix in the sugar and salt. Then rub in the butter or margarine. Make a well in the centre and stir in the yeast liquid with the lightly beaten egg. Mix with a large wooden spoon or fork until the dough leaves the sides of the bowl clean, then turn out on to a lightly floured counter. Knead for about 10 minutes or until the dough is smooth and elastic, sprinkling more flour on the work surface if the dough becomes sticky. Put the dough back into the bowl, cover with a greased polythene bag and leave to rest for 10 minutes.

Take the dough out of the bowl and pummel with knuckles to knock out any large air bubbles. Knead for 1–2 minutes, then shape into a loaf or rolls.

To make a crown loaf: divide the dough into eight equal portions and roll each on the counter or between hands into a smooth ball. Then use seven to form a ring in a greased 8"

(20cm) sandwich tin (at least 1″/2·5cm deep) and put the eighth in the centre.

To make a plait: divide the dough into three and roll each portion into a long, thin sausage-like strip. Join all three at one end and plait to the other. Pinch the ends together (or tuck under) and place on a greased baking tray.

Put the tin or tray into a large greased polythene bag and leave in a warm place until the dough has doubled in size (it should spring back when pressed lightly with a floured finger). Remove the bag, brush lightly with milk or beaten egg, and bake in the centre of a preheated oven (450°F / Gas Mark 8 / 230°C) for about 30 minutes (test by rapping the base with your knuckles: if done, it will sound hollow). Cool on a wire rack, then store or pack in a polythene bag.

Makes 1 large crown loaf or plait

WHEATMEAL BREAD

Yeast Liquid:
½oz (15g) fresh yeast (or 2 level teaspoons dried yeast plus 1 teaspoon sugar)
10oz (275ml) hand-hot water

Dough:
8oz (225g) wholewheat flour
8oz (225g) strong white flour
2 teaspoons salt
½oz (15g) lard

Grease a 1lb (450g) loaf tin and a baking tray.

If using dried yeast, mix it with the sugar and 5oz (150ml) of the hand-hot water and leave in a warm place until frothy. Otherwise, dissolve the fresh yeast in the whole quantity of hand-hot water.

Put the flours in a large mixing bowl, mix in the salt, then rub in the lard. Make a well in the centre and mix in the yeast liquid (if using dried yeast, pour in the remaining water at the same time) with a large wooden spoon or fork until the dough leaves the sides of the bowl clean. Then turn out on to a lightly floured counter and knead until smooth and elastic, sprinkling the work surface with more flour if the dough seems sticky. Divide the dough in two and pat or roll half out into a large oblong (its width should equal the length of the tin; its length should be three times the width of the tin). Roll up, swiss-roll style, or fold in three, smooth over the top and tuck the ends under. Fit into greased tin, seam side down.

Divide the remaining dough into 2oz (50g) portions. Shape into rolls (see White Bread recipe), then place on greased baking tray. Put the tin and tray inside a large greased polythene bag and leave in a warm place until the dough has doubled in size. Remove the bag, brush the dough with lightly salted water and bake in the centre of a preheated oven (425°F/Gas Mark 7/ 220°C) for about 30 minutes (bake the rolls on the second shelf from the top for about 20 minutes). Cool on a wire rack.

Makes 1 small loaf and approximately 6 rolls

EASY GRANARY BREAD

Yeast Liquid:	*Dough:*
1 level tablespoon dried yeast	1lb (450g) granary flour
1 teaspoon brown sugar	5oz–6oz (150ml–175ml) water,
5oz (150ml) hand-hot water	hand-hot
(about 110°F/40°C)	1 teaspoon salt
	1oz (25g) butter/margarine

Grease a 2lb (1kg) or two 1lb (450g) tins.

Measure out the dried yeast and put into a small bowl with the brown sugar and 5oz (150ml) of hand-hot water. Mix well, then put in a warm place for about 15 minutes or until frothy.

Put the flour into a large mixing bowl. Blend in the salt and rub in the butter or margarine. Make a well in the centre, then pour in the frothy yeast mixture with an additional 5oz (150ml) of hand-hot water. With a large wooden spoon or fork, mix until the dough leaves the sides of the bowl clean (adding the remaining water if the dough seems dry). Turn out on to a lightly floured counter and knead until smooth and elastic. Put the dough into the greased tin, levelling off and pressing well into the corners (dampen fingers slightly to do this). Cover with a cloth or put into a greased polythene bag and leave in a warm place until the dough has risen to the top of the tin. Then uncover and bake in the centre of a preheated oven (400°F/Gas Mark 6/200°C) for 30 minutes or until the loaf is well browned and sounds hollow when rapped on the base with knuckles. Loosen round the edges of the tin with a knife, then reverse out on to a wire rack. Turn right side up and leave to cool. Store and pack in a polythene bag.

Makes 1 large or 2 small loaves

HAM AND CHEESE LOAF

Yeast Liquid:
½oz (15g) fresh yeast (or 2 level teaspoons dried yeast plus 1 teaspoon sugar)
5oz (150ml) lukewarm water
5oz (150ml) lukewarm milk

Dough:
8oz (225g) strong white flour
8oz (225g) wholewheat flour
1oz (25g) lard
2 teaspoons salt
1 teaspoon sugar

Filling:
1oz (25g) butter
1 medium onion
2 slices ham
3oz (75g) mature cheddar cheese

Grease a small ring mould (9″/23cm in diameter).

Melt the butter in a frying pan, then add the onion and ham, chopped finely. Cook over gentle heat until the onion is golden brown. (Stir occasionally to keep the mixture from sticking.) Then turn out on to a plate and leave to cool. Grate the cheese and put it on a plate to dry out slightly.

If using dried yeast, mix it in a small bowl with the sugar and 5oz (150ml) of hand-hot water. Leave in a warm place until frothy. If using fresh yeast, put the water and milk into a saucepan and heat to lukewarm. Then take off the heat, add the yeast and stir until completely dissolved.

Put the flours in a large mixing bowl, add the salt and sugar, then rub in the lard. Make a well in the centre and tip in the yeast liquid (if using dried yeast, add the lukewarm milk at this stage) and mix with a wooden spoon or fork until the dough leaves the sides of the bowl clean. Turn out on to a lightly floured counter and knead until the dough is smooth and elastic (sprinkling more flour on the work surface if the dough seems sticky). Put back into the bowl, cover with a greased polythene bag and leave until the dough has doubled in size. Turn the dough out on to a lightly floured counter and pummel with knuckles to knock out any large air bubbles. Then knead for a minute or two and roll out into a large rectangle (about 12"/30cm x 9"/23cm). Spread with the ham and onion mixture and sprinkle with the grated cheese. Roll up from the long side like a swiss roll and pinch the edges together to seal (dampen first). Then roll lightly on the counter with tips of fingers until it is long and thin (about 21"/53cm) and will just fit inside the ring mould. Dampen the ends and pinch together to seal completely. Then gently fit into the mould. Put the tin inside a greased polythene bag and leave until the dough has risen to a gentle curve just above the top of the tin. Remove the bag, brush the dough with milk or lightly salted water and bake in the centre of a preheated oven (425°F / Gas Mark 7 / 220°C) for about 30 minutes. Gently loosen round the inside and outside edges of the tin with a knife and reverse out on to a wire rack. Stand right way up, cover with a clean tea towel and leave to cool. Store and pack in a polythene bag.

Makes 1 good-sized round loaf

CHEESE AND ONION PLAIT

Yeast Liquid:
1oz (25g) fresh yeast
1 (1oz/25g) ascorbic acid
  tablet
8oz (225ml) lukewarm milk

Dough:
1lb (450g) strong white flour
1 teaspoon salt
1 teaspoon sugar
2oz (50g) butter or margarine
1 standard egg

Filling:
2oz (50g) butter
2 large onions
4oz (100g) cheddar cheese, grated

Grease a baking tray.

Melt the butter in a large frying pan and, when foaming, add the onions, chopped finely. Sauté until the onions are soft and golden brown, then put to one side to cool.

Crush the ascorbic acid tablet to a fine powder and dissolve with the yeast in the lukewarm milk. Stir until completely dissolved. Put the flour, salt and sugar into a large mixing bowl and rub in the butter or margarine. Beat the egg lightly and stir into the dry ingredients with the yeast liquid. Mix with a wooden spoon or fork until the dough leaves the sides of the bowl clean, then turn out on to a lightly floured counter. Knead firmly until the dough is smooth and elastic (this takes about 5 minutes). Put the dough back into the bowl and cover with cling film or a greased polythene bag. Leave to rest for 10 minutes. Then return the dough to the work surface and pummel with knuckles to knock out any large air bubbles. Knead lightly back into shape.

Pat or roll the dough out into two rectangles measuring 6″ (15cm) x 4½″ (11cm). Put a thin strip of the onion mixture down the centre of each one and cover with grated cheese. Cut diagonal strips in the dough down either side of the filling. Then plait the strips over it, taking care to cover the filling completely. Pinch the ends of the plait together and fold up or under. Place carefully on greased tray and put inside a large greased polythene bag. Leave in a warm place until the dough has doubled in size. Remove the bag, brush with beaten egg or milk and bake in the centre of a preheated oven (400°F / Gas Mark 6 / 200°C) for 25–30 minutes. Cool on a wire rack. Store and pack in a polythene bag.

Makes 2 large plaits

HUNGARIAN COFFEE CAKE

The name might seem misleading for this cake contains no coffee at all. It is meant, instead, to accompany a steaming hot cup of coffee.

Yeast Liquid:
1oz (25g) fresh yeast
1 (1oz/25g) ascorbic acid
   tablet
8oz (225ml) lukewarm milk

Dough:
1lb (450g) strong white flour
2oz (50g) butter or margarine
1 standard egg
1 teaspoon salt
1 teaspoon sugar

Filling:
2oz (50g) butter
4oz (100g) caster sugar
2oz (50g) raisins
1oz–2oz (25g–50g) chopped walnuts
1½ teaspoons ground cinnamon

Grease a large ring mould (9″/23cm in diameter) or large tube pan.

Crush the ascorbic acid to a fine powder and dissolve with the yeast in the lukewarm milk.

Put the flour in a large mixing bowl with the sugar and salt. Rub in the butter or margarine. Make a well in the centre and pour in the yeast liquid with the egg, lightly beaten. Mix with a wooden fork or spoon until the dough leaves the sides of the bowl clean. Turn out on to a lightly floured counter and knead until smooth and elastic (sprinkling the work surface with more flour if the dough seems sticky). Shape the dough into a ball, return to the bowl and cover with a greased polythene bag. Leave to rest for 10 minutes. Then take out and pummel with knuckles to knock out large air bubbles. Knead lightly back into shape.

Melt the butter in a small saucepan and put to one side. Mix the sugar, cinnamon and chopped walnuts together in a bowl. Shape the dough into small balls (about the size of walnuts) and roll each one first in the melted butter and then in the cinnamon/ sugar mixture. Build up layers of cinnamon-covered balls in the greased ring mould, sprinkling a few raisins between each layer. Put the filled tin into a greased polythene bag and leave in a warm place until the dough has doubled in size. Then remove the bag and bake in the centre of a preheated oven (375°F/ Gas Mark 5/190°C) for 35–40 minutes. Loosen round the inside and outside edges with a knife and reverse on to a wire rack. Leave the tin on for about 5 minutes so that the syrup coats the sides of the cake. Then remove and leave to cool. Store and pack in a polythene bag. When ready to serve, pull pieces of the cake apart with your fingers. Serve as it is or with butter.

Makes 1 large cake

Quick Breads

WHOLEWHEAT IRISH SODA BREAD

6oz (175g) plain flour	1 teaspoon bicarbonate of soda
10oz (275g) wholewheat flour	2 teaspoons cream of tartar
1 teaspoon sugar	1oz (25g) butter
1 teaspoon salt	½ pint (275ml) milk

Grease and generously flour a baking tray.
Preheat oven to 400°F / Gas Mark 6 / 200°C.

Sift the plain flour, sugar, salt, bicarbonate of soda and cream of tartar into a large mixing bowl. Add the wholewheat flour and rub in the butter. Make a well in the centre, then pour in the milk. Mix to a soft dough with a round-topped knife or fork, adding more milk if necessary.

Turn out on to a lightly floured surface and knead gently until the dough is smooth. Then shape into a round about 7″ (18cm) in diameter. Mark into four equal sections with the back of a knife and place on greased baking tray. Brush lightly with milk or salted water. Bake on the second shelf from the top of the oven for 30–40 minutes or until the bread sounds hollow when rapped on the base with knuckles. Cool on a wire rack (if you prefer a softer crust, cover with a clean tea towel while cooling). Store and pack in a polythene bag. This bread doesn't keep well and should be eaten within a day or two of making.

Makes 1 round loaf

APPLE, CHEDDAR AND WALNUT BREAD

8oz (225g) plain flour
1 teaspoon salt
twist of black pepper
1 teaspoon bicarbonate of soda
1 teaspoon baking powder
1 teaspoon ground cinnamon
4oz (100g) sugar

4oz (100g) mature cheddar cheese
2oz (50g) chopped walnuts
1 medium cooking apple (about 8oz/225g in weight)
3oz (75g) butter
2 standard eggs

3oz (75ml) milk

Grease a 2lb (1kg) loaf tin.
Preheat oven to 350°F / Gas Mark 4 / 180°C.

Sift the flour, salt, twist of black pepper, bicarbonate of soda, baking powder, cinnamon and sugar into a large mixing bowl. Grate the cheddar and add with the walnuts, chopped finely.

Then peel, core and chop the apple into very small dice. Toss lightly in the flour mixture.

Melt the butter and beat the eggs lightly. Make a well in the dry ingredients and pour in the melted butter, beaten eggs and the milk. Gradually draw in the flour from around the sides until it has all been blended in (be careful not to beat).

Pour the batter (this will be quite lumpy) into greased tin, spreading into the corners and levelling off with the back of a spoon. Bake in the centre of preheated oven for 60–70 minutes (or until a toothpick inserted into the centre comes out clean). Loosen round the edges with a knife, then reverse out on to a wire rack. Turn right side up and leave to cool. Store and pack in a polythene bag. Serve sliced and spread with butter. (This loaf keeps well and is always improved if kept for 24 hours before cutting.)

Makes 1 large loaf

CRUNCHY GRANOLA BREAD

4oz (100g) butter, at room
    temperature
2oz (50g) soft brown sugar
2 level tablespoons treacle
1 large egg
4oz (100g) wholewheat flour
4oz (100g) plain flour

1 teaspoon bicarbonate of soda
1 teaspoon baking powder
¼ teaspoon salt
8oz (225g) plain yogurt
6oz (175g) crunchy oat break-
    fast cereal with raisins

Grease a 2lb (1kg) loaf tin.
Preheat oven to 350°F / Gas Mark 4 / 180°C.

Cream the butter and sugar together in a large bowl until light and fluffy. Blend in the treacle and then the egg, lightly beaten.

Sift the flours, bicarbonate of soda, baking powder and salt on to a plate or sheet of greaseproof paper (tipping the bran which remains in the sieve on top). Add to the creamed mixture alternately with the yogurt (whisk this first with a fork until completely smooth). Then blend in the crunchy breakfast cereal and stir only until it has all been mixed in (too much stirring will produce large air bubbles in the bread).

Pour into greased tin, spreading the batter into the corners and levelling off the top. Bake in the centre of the oven for an hour or until a toothpick inserted in the centre comes out clean. Loosen round the edges with a knife, then reverse out on to a wire rack. Turn right side up and leave to cool. Store and pack in a polythene bag. Serve sliced and spread with butter.

Makes 1 large loaf

WHEATMEAL SCONES

3oz (75g) plain flour   1½oz (40g) sugar
5oz (150g) wholewheat flour   large pinch of salt
3 teaspoons baking powder   2oz (50g) butter
5oz (150ml) milk

Grease and generously flour a large baking tray.
Preheat oven to 450°F / Gas Mark 8 / 230°C.

Sift the plain flour, baking powder, sugar and salt together into a large mixing bowl. Add the wholewheat flour and rub in the butter until the mixture resembles coarse breadcrumbs. Make a well in the centre and pour in the milk. Mix to a soft dough with a fork or round-topped knife.

Turn the dough out on to a lightly floured counter and knead for half a minute or until smooth. Shape into a small round (about 6″/15cm in diameter) and mark into six equal triangles with a floured knife. Place on greased tray and bake on the second shelf from the top of the oven for 20–25 minutes or until lightly browned. Cool on a wire rack. Store and pack in a polythene bag. When ready to serve, separate the triangles, split them in half and spread with butter.

Makes 6 large scones

CHEESE AND BACON SCONES

2 gammon rashers (or 4 streaky bacon rashers)	½ teaspoon salt
	twist of black pepper
4oz (100g) mature cheddar	½ teaspoon dry mustard
8oz (225g) self-raising flour*	2oz (50g) butter or margarine
	5oz (150ml) milk

Grease and flour a large baking tray.
Preheat oven to 425°F / Gas Mark 7 / 220°C.

Cook the bacon until crisp, then drain on absorbent kitchen paper. Grate the cheese and put to one side.

Sift the flour, salt, pepper and mustard together into a mixing bowl. Rub in the butter until the mixture resembles coarse breadcrumbs, then blend in the grated cheese and bacon (crumbled into small pieces). Make a well in the centre and pour in the milk. Mix until the dough leaves the sides of the bowl clean.

Turn out on to a lightly floured counter and knead lightly until smooth. Roll out to a ½" (1cm) thickness and stamp out rounds with a biscuit cutter (any size you like). Or roll out to a ¼" (·50cm) thickness and cut into finger lengths. Place on prepared tray, brush with milk and bake on the second shelf from the top of the oven for 12–15 minutes (or until golden brown). Dust with flour and cool on a wire rack. Store and pack in polythene bag. Serve with butter or on their own.

Makes about 30 miniature or 10 large scones

* For a 'nutty' flavour, substitute wholewheat self-raising flour instead.

Recipes for the following are found in other parts of the book: Yorkshire Spice Bread (p. 228), Currant Buns (p. 227).

5

CROUSTADES, SANDWICHES AND STUFFED VEGETABLES

At this point, young Bingo came up. I hadn't seen him look so jaunty for days.

'I've just been superintending the packing of the lunch-basket, Bertie,' he said. 'I stood over the butler and saw that there was no nonsense.'

'All pretty sound?' I asked, relieved.

'All indubitably sound.'

'No carrots?'

'No carrots,' said young Bingo. 'There's ham sand-wiches,' he proceeded, a strange, soft light in his eyes, 'and tongue sandwiches and potted meat sandwiches and game sandwiches and hard-boiled eggs and lobster and a cold chicken and sardines and a cake and a couple of bottles of Bollinger and some old brandy.'

'It has the right ring,' I said. 'And if we want a bite to eat after that, of course we can go to the pub.'

from *Jeeves and the Old School Chum*

One item would have been conspicuously absent from the picnic basket today had it not been for the Earl of Sandwich's keen love of gambling. Unwilling to leave the gaming tables even to eat, he ordered his dinner to be brought to him. Thick slices of meat arrived between two trenchers of bread and established a precedent which has been followed ever since.

The basic formula is simple, but the end result has infinite variations. There are those who insist that the bread should be cut paper-thin and others who slice it as thick as doorsteps. Still others refuse to eat sandwiches altogether, considering them half a meal or not half good enough. The Scandinavians prefer them open, the Americans like them toasted and the French favour them crusty. The only thing they all agree on is their suitability for picnics!

Croustade, Sandwich, and Stuffed Vegetable Tips

***** If making sandwiches in advance, wrap them first in cling film or a polythene bag and then in a damp tea towel. This will keep them moist until needed.

***** Crusty loaves and rolls should be brushed inside and out with melted butter and baked in a moderate oven for about 30 minutes before filling (cool them slightly first). This makes them shiny and crisp and keeps them from becoming soggy when filled.

***** Croustades, 'crostini' and melba toast can be made in advance and if stored in a polythene bag or tightly closed tin will stay crisp for at least a week. Add the filling just before leaving and pack on a plate (then cover with foil) or in a foil-lined tin.

***** As a general rule, sandwiches and rolls which need to be kept moist should be packed in a plastic container; those, like croustades, which need to be kept crisp should be packed in a tin.

***** When stuffing vegetables with a high water content (cucumber, tomatoes, courgettes, etc.), 'dégorger' them first by slicing open and sprinkling generously with salt. Leave for 30 minutes then pour off any liquid and wipe dry with absorbent kitchen paper. Stand on a double layer of kitchen paper while filling to absorb any excess moisture.

WHOLEWHEAT OR GRANARY CROUSTADES

These provide a wonderfully crisp base for any number of fillings. They can be made in advance and if stored in a tightly closed tin or polythene bag will retain their crispness for a week at least. For best results, they should be filled a few hours before the picnic and not the day before.

> 8 large slices of wholewheat or granary bread*
> 1oz–2oz (25g–50g) butter

Patty tins
Preheat oven to 350°F / Gas Mark 4 / 180°C.

Melt the butter and put to one side. Remove the crusts and cut out a large circle from each slice of bread. Brush both sides with melted butter, then fit each round into one section of the patty tins.

Bake in the centre of preheated oven for 30 minutes to an hour or until the croustades are crisp and well browned. Take out and cool on a wire rack. Store in a polythene bag or tin.

* White bread can also be used and is more suitable for delicately-flavoured fillings (e.g. asparagus).

TUNA FILLING

1 (7oz/200g) tin of tuna	1 large hard-boiled egg
1 large stalk celery	a good squeeze of lemon juice
1 tablespoon of chopped pimento (or chopped stuffed olives)	salt and black pepper
	3–4 tablespoons mayonnaise
	paprika or chopped parsley

Drain the tuna well, then put into a bowl and flake with a fork. Chop the celery and the hard-boiled egg finely and mix in. Then

74

add the chopped pimento (or stuffed olives), a good squeeze of lemon juice, salt and freshly ground black pepper. Bind together with mayonnaise (being careful not to add too much or it will make the mixture soggy).

Fill each croustade with a dollop of the tuna. Sprinkle with paprika or chopped parsley, arrange on a plate and cover with foil (or put into a foil-tined tin).

CRUSTY ROLLS

8–10 small crusty rolls   1oz–2oz (25g–50g) butter

Grease a large baking tray.
Preheat oven to 350°F / Gas Mark 4 / 180°C.

With a sharp knife, cut a large, deep circle out of the top of each roll (about ½"/1cm from the outside edge all the way around). Then slice the inside of the 'caps' off so that they are completely flat (the bread you cut off can be used for bread-crumbs at some other time). Melt the butter and brush the rolls (and the 'caps') generously with it, inside and out. Place the rolls and 'caps' on the baking tray and bake in the centre of the oven for 30 minutes to an hour, or until quite crisp. Take out and fill immediately or leave to cool. If kept in a tin or polythene bag, these will keep for about a week.

ASPARAGUS FILLING

1oz (25g) butter
2 level tablespoons flour
5oz (150ml) milk
2 teaspoons dried parsley
3 large hard-boiled eggs

1 (12oz/340g) tin asparagus
   spears
salt and white pepper
chopped parsley (fresh or
   dried)

Melt the butter in a saucepan, stir in the flour and cook for 1 minute. Take off the heat, add the milk gradually then cook over moderate heat, stirring constantly, until the mixture thickens and boils. Chop the hard-boiled egg finely and add to the sauce with the dried parsley. Season to taste with salt and white pepper. Drain the asparagus, reserving the juice. Chop into small pieces and blend into the sauce, adding just enough of the juice to give it the consistency of single cream.

Fill each roll with a few spoonfuls of the asparagus mixture. Sprinkle with chopped parsley, then put a 'cap' on each one, slightly at an angle. Put into a foil-lined tin, cover with a lid and refrigerate until needed. (These can be made the day before.)

Makes 8–10 small filled rolls

PICNIC LOAF

1 small crusty white loaf   1oz–2oz (25g–50g) butter
   (or French baguette)

Preheat oven to 350°F / Gas Mark 4 / 180°C.

Slice the loaf horizontally about two-thirds of the way up. Take off the top third (the lid). Then remove most of the bread in the bottom two-thirds, leaving a 1″ (2·5cm) layer all the way around. Melt the butter and brush the loaf and lid generously with it, inside and out. Put both on a baking tray and bake in the centre of the oven for 30 minutes to an hour or until quite crisp (but not dried out). Take out, put in the filling, replace the lid and wrap tightly in aluminium foil. (Or the loaf can be cooled, stored in a polythene bag and filled later.)

If using a French baguette, follow the same method, but cut the loaf exactly in half horizontally.

SALMON AND CUCUMBER FILLING

As this filling is quite moist, the crisp, crusty baguette is the best to use with it.

¾ large cucumber
1 (7½oz/211g) tin red or pink
    salmon
4–5 tablespoons mayonnaise
salt and freshly ground black
    pepper
good squeeze of lemon juice

Wash the outside of the cucumber, wipe dry and cut into small dice. Put on a large plate, sprinkle generously with salt and leave for 30 minutes. Then pour the water off and dry the cucumber with absorbent kitchen paper.

Drain the salmon well, then put into a bowl and flake with a fork. Add the lemon juice, diced cucumber and just enough mayonnaise to bind it together without making it too moist. Season to taste with salt and black pepper. Then use to fill the picnic loaf, replace the lid and wrap tightly in foil. (If you find yourself with a rather large loaf and not enough filling, line the loaf first with well-dried lettuce leaves.) This must be made the day of the picnic.

Makes 1 good-sized filled loaf

PAN BAGNA

This traditional Niçoise sandwich takes you one step closer to the Mediterranean on a hot summer's day.

1 small crusty white loaf
olive or vegetable oil

Filling:
4 large ripe tomatoes
4oz (100g) sliced cheese
8–10 slices of salami
1 green pepper
salt and pepper
anchovy fillets

Cut the loaf in half horizontally. Brush the inside of both halves with oil. Wash, dry and slice the tomatoes thinly. Do the same with the green pepper, slicing it across rather than lengthwise. Put a layer of salami slices on the bottom half of the loaf, then one of tomatoes, green pepper and finally one of cheese. Sprinkle

77

with salt and pepper and top with a few anchovy fillets if you like. Replace the top half and wrap the loaf tightly in foil.

Serves 6–8

PAIN PERDU

This is an excellent way of using up slightly stale bread (which might otherwise be 'perdu'). They should be made on the day of the picnic.

8 slices of wholewheat   1oz–2oz (25g–50g) butter
  or white bread

Grease a small baking tray or tin.
Preheat oven to 350°F / Gas Mark 4 / 180°C.

Cut the crusts off the bread, then use a rolling pin to flatten each slice as thinly as possible (do this gently or the bread will split). Melt the butter and brush both sides of each slice lightly with it. Put a small amount of filling in the centre of the bread, then roll up like a swiss roll and put, seam side down and close together, in the baking tin. Brush with any remaining butter and bake in the centre of the oven for 30–40 minutes or until crisp and lightly browned.

TOMATO AND CHEESE FILLING

4 ripe tomatoes   mayonnaise
2oz (50g) cheddar cheese   salt and pepper

Wash and dry the tomatoes. Cut into quarters, remove the seeds and cut again into small pieces. Chop the cheese into very small dice. Spread a thin layer of mayonnaise on one side of each slice and top this with a sprinkling of tomatoes and cheese. Season with salt and pepper. Roll up tightly, then put, seam side down and close together, into a greased baking tin. Bake as above.

CHEESE AND HAM FILLING

2 slices of cooked ham   3oz (75g) cheddar cheese

Cut the ham and cheese into small dice. Put a small amount of each in the centre of each slice, then roll up and bake as above.

Makes 8 'pain perdu'

CROSTINI

8 slices of white or brown   or 4–6 tablespoons olive or
    bread   vegetable oil
           2oz–3oz (50g–75g) butter

Remove the crusts and cut the bread into rounds (of any size). Heat the oil or butter in a large frying pan and when sizzling, add the bread. Fry on both sides until crisp and well browned. Then cool on a wire rack. (If stored in a tightly closed polythene bag or tin these will stay crisp for a week at least.)

MELBA TOAST

8 thin slices of white or brown bread*

Remove the crusts and cut each slice diagonally into four quarters. Spread out on a baking tray and bake in a slow oven (325°F / Gas Mark 3 / 170°C) for an hour or until crisp and lightly browned. Cool, then store in a tin or polythene bag.

* Not cut too thinly or the melba toast will crumble easily.

PATE AND BACON SPREAD

8 medium crostini or 16
  quarters of melba toast
1oz (25g) soft butter

3oz–4oz (75g–100g) smooth
  pâté
4 rashers of streaky bacon
chopped dried parsley

Spread the crostini or melba toast with a thin layer of butter,
then cover with the pâté. Cook the bacon until crisp, then drain
on a piece of absorbent kitchen paper. Crumble or cut into small
pieces and sprinkle over the pâté-covered toast with a small
amount of dried parsley. Pack in a tin or an aluminium-foil
container.

Serves 6–8

WHOLEWHEAT CREPES

A speciality of Brittany, these are specially toasted for picnics
until they are crisp and well browned.

Batter:
8oz (225g) wholewheat flour
½ teaspoon salt
¾ pint (425ml) milk (or milk
  and water mixed)

2 eggs, beaten
black pepper
vegetable oil or butter

Sift the flour, salt and pepper into a mixing bowl. Make a well
in the centre and gradually blend in the beaten eggs and milk.
Pour into a jug and let it rest for at least 30 minutes.

Heat a tablespoon of olive or vegetable oil or a good knob
of butter in a small heavy frying pan. When very hot, pour in
just enough batter to cover the bottom of the pan. Cook quickly
for several minutes, flip over and cook the other side. Lift with
a fish slice on to a square of absorbent kitchen paper. If not
using straight away, layer the crêpes with squares of greaseproof

paper and keep in a tightly tied polythene bag (if refrigerated these will keep for several weeks, and, if frozen, for several months).

Makes about 10–12 good-sized crêpes

RATATOUILLE FILLING

1 medium aubergine	large pinch of sugar
1 large green pepper	½ teaspoon dried mixed herbs
3 large tomatoes	1 tablespoon grated Parmesan
1 large onion	cheese
1½oz (40g) butter	salt and pepper to taste

Wipe the aubergine, cut in half lengthwise, score the surface with a knife and sprinkle with salt. Leave for half an hour, then wipe dry with absorbent kitchen paper. Cut into small pieces. Blanch the pepper quickly in boiling water, then dry and remove the seeds and pith. Cut into small dice. Wipe the tomatoes and cut into small sections (it's not necessary to peel them but be careful to reserve all their juices). Peel the onion and dice finely.

Melt the butter in a large frying pan and add the chopped onion. Cook until soft, then add the remaining vegetables. Toss well in the butter, then cook over moderate heat until the mixture becomes thick. Add the dried herbs, salt and pepper to taste and the Parmesan cheese. Mix well and take off the heat.

Put a thin strip of filling down the centre of each crêpe (if they're quite large, cut them in half and fold up like a parcel) and roll up, tucking the ends under. Place on a greased baking tray and bake in a hot oven (400°F / Gas Mark 6 / 200°C) for about 30–40 minutes or until the crêpes are nicely browned and very crisp. *To serve hot:* take straight from the oven, wrap in a double layer of foil and pack in an insulated bag or a thick towel. Or, if small crêpes, pack in an aluminium-foil container, put the lid on tightly and wrap in several tea towels. *To serve cold:* cool, wrap in foil and pack.

VOL AU VENTS

Though these are traditionally served hot, they taste quite delicious cold and travel well in a biscuit tin or long plastic container.

1 (14oz/400g) packet frozen
  puff pastry (or home-made
  puff pastry)

Grease a large baking tray.
Preheat oven to 450°F / Gas Mark 8 / 230°C.

Let the pastry thaw until just pliable enough to handle (be careful not to let it get too soft). Roll out thinly on a lightly floured counter. Then cut out rounds with a biscuit cutter, and lift on to baking tray. Then with a slightly smaller cutter, mark a centre circle on each one which can be taken out after baking and used as a lid. Brush with beaten egg and bake until well risen and golden. Cool on a wire rack. (If the dough gets warm while rolling, chill the rounds on the baking tray for a short time before baking.) These freeze well and will stay fresh up to a week if kept in a polythene bag in the refrigerator.

Makes about 12 large or 24 small vol au vents

CHICKEN A LA KING FILLING

2 large cooked chicken breasts	4oz (100ml) chicken stock
½ large green pepper	salt and pepper to taste
4oz (100g) button mushrooms	1 tablespoon sherry (optional)
1oz (25g) butter	chopped parsley (fresh or
2 level tablespoons flour	dried)
5oz (150ml) milk	

Remove the skin and chop the chicken into small pieces. Blanch the pepper quickly in boiling water, remove the pith and seeds, then cut into very small dice. Wipe the mushrooms and cut into small pieces.

Melt the butter in a large saucepan. Add the mushrooms and green pepper and cook over moderate heat until soft. Then stir in the flour, cook for 1 minute and take off the heat. Gradually mix in the milk, return to the heat and stir until the mixture thickens and boils. Slowly add the chicken stock, the sherry, and season to taste with salt and pepper. Fold in the chicken, check the seasoning again and take off the heat. Leave to cool, and if too thick add a small amount of milk or cream. Then fill the vol au vent cases and sprinkle with dried or freshly chopped parsley.

Sufficient to fill 10–12 large or 20–24 small vol au vents

Sandwich Fillings

EGG SALAD

4 large eggs	or chopped chives
4 tablespoons mayonnaise	1 teaspoon French mustard
1½oz (40g) melted butter	2 stalks celery
2 teaspoons grated onion	salt and pepper

Cook the eggs until hard, then rinse well under cold water and peel. Chop finely, and put into a mixing bowl with the mayonnaise, melted butter, grated onion (or chives) and mustard. Add the celery, chopped into small dice. Blend all the ingredients together well and season to taste with salt and pepper.

This is quite a soft mixture and ideally suited to large round baps or wholewheat finger rolls. (It is not quite as likely to escape out the sides of them as it is from ordinary sandwiches or crusty rolls.)

Sufficient to fill 8 large baps or finger rolls

CHICKEN SALAD

4 large cooked chicken breasts
2 large stalks celery
salt and pepper
good squeeze of lemon juice
1 tablespoon white wine or
  tarragon vinegar

2 tablespoons olive or
  vegetable oil
½ teaspoon French mustard
½ teaspoon sugar
4 tablespoons mayonnaise

Take the skin off and chop the chicken into small pieces. Put into a bowl with the celery, washed and chopped finely. Sprinkle with salt and pepper, then give a good squeeze of lemon juice. Put the mayonnaise, vinegar, oil, mustard, sugar, salt and pepper into a screw-top jar. Shake vigorously until well blended, then pour over the chicken and toss well (add more mayonnaise if necessary to bind the mixture together). Delicious on white or brown bread, with a crisp lettuce leaf added to each sandwich.

Makes 6–8 sandwiches

TUNA OR SALMON SALAD

1 (7oz/200g) tin of tuna or
  salmon
1 large stalk celery
or ¼ small cucumber
2 tablespoons finely chopped
  onion

1 tablespoon chopped gherkins
  or pickle relish
4 tablespoons mayonnaise
salt and black pepper

Drain the tuna or salmon well, then put into a bowl and flake with a fork. Wash and dry the celery (or cucumber) with absorbent kitchen paper, then chop into small dice. Mix into the fish with the chopped onion, pickle and mayonnaise (add only enough mayonnaise to bind the mixture together). Season to taste with salt and pepper.

DEVILLED HAM FILLING

8oz (225g) cooked ground ham
1 large stalk celery
1 small spring onion
1 teaspoon freshly chopped
   parsley

1 tablespoon chutney
2 teaspoons French mustard
4–6 tablespoons mayonnaise
large pinch sugar
salt and pepper

Wash the celery and spring onion, then chop finely. Put into a bowl with the ground ham. Mix the chutney, mustard, sugar, parsley and four tablespoons of mayonnaise together, then pour over the ham. Blend in well, adding more mayonnaise if necessary to bind the mixture together. Season to taste with salt and pepper. Especially good on melba toast or toasted wholewheat muffins.

Sufficient to fill 4–6 sandwiches or 6–8 muffin halves

WINDSOR FILLING

4oz (100g) cooked chicken
4oz (100g) cooked ham
1oz (25g) soft butter
4–6 tablespoons mayonnaise

sprinkling of chopped parsley
squeeze of lemon juice
salt and pepper

Remove the skin and chop the chicken into small pieces. Shred the ham finely. Soften the butter in a bowl and gradually blend in 4 tablespoons of mayonnaise. Then mix in the chicken, ham, chopped parsley, lemon juice and season to taste with salt and pepper. (Add more mayonnaise to bind the mixture together if necessary.)

Sufficient to fill 4–6 sandwiches

AVOCADO AND BACON FILLING

1 large ripe avocado
3 rashers streaky bacon
2 teaspoons lemon juice
½ teaspoon sugar
¼ teaspoon French mustard
2 teaspoons vegetable or olive oil
2 tablespoons mayonnaise
salt and pepper

Peel the avocado, remove the stone and mash with a fork until smooth. Cook the bacon until crisp, then drain on absorbent kitchen paper. Crumble or cut into small pieces and add to the avocado. Put the lemon juice, sugar, mustard, oil and mayonnaise into a screw-top jar and shake until well blended. Mix just enough into the avocado/bacon mixture to bind it together, then season to taste with salt and black pepper. Spread on crusty rolls or soft baps. (This must be made the same day as the picnic.)

Sufficient to fill 4–6 small rolls

CREAM CHEESE AND OLIVE SPREAD

4oz (100g) cream cheese
4–8 stuffed green olives
2 tablespoons mayonnaise
2 tablespoons milk or cream

Soften the cream cheese in a bowl and blend in just enough milk or cream to give it a spreading consistency. Chop the olives finely and mix in with the mayonnaise and a good sprinkling of salt and pepper. Spread on crostini or melba toast and decorate with additional chopped olives.

Sufficient to fill 4–6 sandwiches or spread on 8–10 slices of toast

PEANUT BUTTER AND BANANA

Though adults recoil in horror at this, young picnickers adore it.

86

crunchy peanut butter   white or brown bread
sliced bananas

Spread one slice of bread generously with peanut butter, then top with thinly sliced banana and a second slice of bread. Press down firmly, cut in half and wrap in cling film.

Special Sandwiches

CLUB SANDWICHES

slices of white or brown bread   tomato slices
  (or toast)   crisp lettuce
slices of cooked chicken   mayonnaise
rashers of crisp bacon   salt and pepper
        soft butter

Make up each sandwich by spreading one slice of bread or toast with butter and the other with mayonnaise. On top of the buttered slice, put a few pieces of chicken, slices of tomato and a bacon rasher, cut in half or quarters. Sprinkle with salt and pepper, top with a lettuce leaf and cover with the second slice of bread. Press down firmly, then wrap in cling film. Pack a sharp knife with the sandwiches so that they can be cut just before serving.

BACON, LETTUCE AND TOMATO

slices of white or brown bread   mayonnaise
  (or toast)   lettuce
ripe tomatoes   salt and black pepper
rashers of crisp bacon   soft butter

Make up each sandwich by spreading one slice of bread or toast with butter and the other with mayonnaise. Cover the buttered bread with thin slices of tomato, then sprinkle with salt and black pepper. Cover with bacon rashers, cut into halves or quarters and top with a crisp lettuce leaf. Put the second slice of bread (spread with mayonnaise) on top and press down firmly, then wrap in cling film. Cut with a sharp knife just before serving.

CROQUE-MONSIEUR

thin slices of Gruyère cheese
slices of cooked ham
soft butter
white or brown bread

For each sandwich, spread one side of two bread slices with butter. Turn butter side up and cover with a slice of Gruyère cheese and a slice of ham. Top with the second slice of bread (butter side in) and press down firmly. Melt an ounce of butter in a frying pan and, when foaming, add the sandwiches. Cook over moderate heat until golden brown on both sides. Take out and trim the crusts off neatly. Cut in halves or quarters and wrap in foil.

CORNED BEEF ON RYE

slices of corned beef
mustard
soft butter
rye bread

For each sandwich spread one slice of rye bread with butter and another with mustard. Slice the corned beef thinly and pile several pieces on one slice of the rye bread. Top with the second slice and press down firmly. Cut in half, then wrap in cling film.

CRABMEAT SANDWICHES

crabmeat (fresh or tinned)
home-made mayonnaise
squeeze of lemon juice
clove of garlic
salt and freshly ground black
  pepper
mustard and cress
brown bread
butter

Put the crabmeat into a bowl and blend in the mayonnaise and lemon juice. Crush the garlic to a smooth paste in a small amount of salt, then mix in well. Season to taste with salt and pepper. Make up sandwiches with the brown bread and butter, putting a good dollop of crabmeat and sprinkling of mustard and cress in each one. Wrap in cling film and chill until needed.

Other Sandwich Suggestions

Thinly sliced cucumber / brown bread
Smoked salmon / cream cheese / brown bread
Egg / cress / brown bread
Sliced chicken or turkey / lettuce / mayonnaise
Sardines / squeeze of lemon juice / brown bread
Sliced ham / mustard / white or brown bread
Cream cheese / chopped walnuts or chopped dates /
white or brown bread
Asparagus spears rolled in slices of brown bread
(with crusts removed)
Cheddar cheese / chutney / white or brown bread
Cream cheese / pineapple (tinned) or peaches /
white or brown bread
Cheese / tomato slices / lettuce / white or brown bread
Bacon / soft baps

The Carpenter said nothing but, 'The butter's spread
too thick!'

from *Through the Looking Glass*

Stuffed Vegetables

STUFFED CUCUMBERS

1 large cucumber or 2 small

Wash the cucumber and dry well with absorbent kitchen paper. Cut across into 2″ (5cm) pieces and stand upright. Using a small teaspoon, scoop out the inside, leaving about an eighth of an inch (·25cm) all around and being careful not to cut through to the bottom. Sprinkle generously with salt and leave on a plate for at least 30 minutes. Pour the water off and dry well with kitchen paper. Stand on a double layer of kitchen paper and fill with one of the following:

CREAM CHEESE AND PINEAPPLE FILLING

3oz (75g) cream cheese
5oz (150g) diced tinned pine-apple*
2 teaspoons sugar (or to taste)

Soften the cream cheese with a fork, then blend in the diced pineapple (well drained), reserving some for decoration. Add sugar to taste. Put a large dollop of the mixture into the centre of each cucumber and top with a pineapple segment. Line a plastic container with absorbent kitchen paper and put the filled cucumber pieces in carefully. Cover with a lid and refrigerate until needed.

* Don't be tempted to use fresh pineapple as it will react with the cream cheese to produce a very sour taste.

CREAM CHEESE/RAISIN/APPLE FILLING

3oz (75g) cream cheese
1 tablespoon milk
1 teaspoon lemon juice
1 teaspoon sugar

2 tablespoons raisins or
  currants
1 medium (dessert) apple

Soften the cream cheese with a fork, then gradually blend in the lemon juice, milk, sugar and raisins. Wash the apple, dry well, then core and chop into small dice. Add to the bowl and mix well. Then use to fill the cucumber chunks. Pack as above.

STUFFED COURGETTES

4 medium courgettes
1 small onion
2 ripe tomatoes
1oz (25g) butter

1oz (25g) cheddar cheese,
  grated
dried breadcrumbs
salt

Cut the courgettes in half lengthwise and sprinkle with salt. Leave on a plate or piece of absorbent kitchen paper for half an hour, then wipe dry. Carefully cut round the outside edge (leaving about a ¼"/·25cm border all the way round) and scoop out the centres. Peel and chop the onion. Wash the tomatoes and cut into small pieces.

Melt the butter in a frying pan and, when foaming, add the chopped onion, tomatoes and courgette centres. Cook over moderate heat, shaking the pan occasionally to prevent sticking, until the mixture becomes thick. Then use to fill the courgette shells. Place on a baking tray and sprinkle with the grated cheese and breadcrumbs. Bake uncovered for 20–30 minutes at 375°F/Gas Mark 5/190°C. Leave to cool, then pack in a plastic container. If the courgettes are large, cut in half widthwise so that they are easier to eat.

Makes 8 stuffed courgettes

STUFFED POTATOES

4 large potatoes

Scrub the potatoes well and bake at 400°F / Gas Mark 6 / 200°C for an hour or until cooked through. Leave until cool enough to handle.

BACON, CHIVES AND SOUR CREAM FILLING

4 large baked potatoes
4 streaky bacon rashers
5oz (150ml) commercially
  soured cream

1 tablespoon chopped fresh
  chives or 2 tablespoons
  chopped dried chives
2 tablespoons soft butter

salt and black pepper

Cook the bacon until crisp, then drain on absorbent kitchen paper. Crumble or cut into very small pieces and put to one side.
  Cut the baked potatoes in half horizontally or lengthwise. Scoop out the centres (leaving a $\frac{1}{8}$"/·25cm border around the edge) and put into a bowl. Mash until smooth, then blend in the sour cream and soft butter. Add half the bacon, half the chives and season to taste with salt and black pepper. Mix well, then spoon or pipe the mixture back into the potato shells. Sprinkle with the remaining bacon and chives. Pack in a plastic container or small basket, then cover with a lid or foil. If the potatoes are cut lengthwise, cut in half (across) again to make them easier to eat. These can be made the day before the picnic but should be refrigerated until needed.

Makes 8 stuffed potatoes

STUFFED TOMATOES

6–8 small firm tomatoes   salt

Wash the tomatoes and wipe dry with absorbent kitchen paper.
Slice the tops off and scoop out the insides. Sprinkle with salt
and invert on a plate for at least half an hour. Then shake off
excess juice, turn right side up and fill.

FRENCH BEAN VINAIGRETTE FILLING

8oz (225g) french beans (fresh   3 tablespoons olive or
  or frozen)   vegetable oil
½ teaspoon French mustard   large pinch of dried mixed
1 teaspoon caster sugar   herbs
1 tablespoon wine vinegar   salt and freshly ground pepper

Put a small amount of water into a saucepan, sprinkle with salt
and bring to a rolling boil. Add the beans and cook quickly for
about 5 minutes or until just tender. Pour into a colander and
drain well. Then chop into 1″ (2·5cm) lengths and put into a
bowl.
   Put the mustard, sugar, vinegar, oil, dried herbs, salt and
pepper into a screw-top jar. Shake vigorously until well blended,
then pour over the beans and toss well. Stuff the tomatoes with
the mixture. Pack in a plastic container lined with absorbent
kitchen paper or put on a plate or into a small basket and cover
with a lid, cling film or foil.

Makes 6–8 small stuffed tomatoes

STUFFED CELERY

6–8 large stalks of celery

ROQUEFORT FILLING

3oz (75g) Roquefort (or any blue cheese)

large pinch of dried onions

3oz (75g) cream cheese

1–2 tablespoons milk or cream

chopped parsley

Put the blue cheese into a medium bowl and soften with a fork. In another bowl, cream the other cheese until soft and gradually blend in the milk or cream. Mix in the blue cheese, dried onions, and whisk until smooth.

Wash the celery and dry well with absorbent kitchen paper. Then fill with the Roquefort mixture and cut into 2″ (5cm) lengths. Put on to a double layer of kitchen paper (to absorb the excess moisture) and refrigerate until needed. Pack in a plastic container lined with kitchen paper. Sprinkle lightly with parsley.

Makes about 18–24 pieces of stuffed celery

STUFFED EGGS

4 large eggs

Boil the eggs for at least five minutes, rinse well under cold water and peel straight away (if they are still slightly warm when you peel them the shells will come off more easily).

To pack stuffed eggs:
Instead of cutting the eggs in half lengthwise, cut them horizontally. Remove the yolks and put each white into a section of the bottom half of an egg carton. Make up the filling, and pipe or spoon into the whites. Close the carton and pack.

DEVILLED EGGS

4 large hard-boiled eggs
3–4 tablespoons mayonnaise
1½ tablespoons mango chutney

large pinch of curry powder
salt and pepper
paprika

Cut the eggs in half horizontally. Fit the whites into an empty egg carton (see above) and put the yolks into a small bowl. Mash well with a fork, then mix in the mayonnaise (adding more if necessary), mango chutney and curry powder. Season to taste with salt and pepper. Then spoon or pipe the mixture into the whites and sprinkle with paprika. Close the carton and refrigerate until needed.

Makes 8 stuffed eggs

Recipes for the following can be found in other parts of the book:
French Toast (p. 279), Toasted Cheese Sandwiches (p. 279),
Crêpes Bretonnes (p. 242).

6

QUICHES, PIZZAS, PIES

Here, with his broad back against the rugged trunk of the willow tree, and half hidden by the soft ferns around him sat a stout, brawny fellow. His head was round as a ball, and covered with a mat of close-clipped curly black hair that grew low down on his forehead. But his crown was shorn as smooth as the palm of one's hand, which, together with his loose robe, cowl and string of beads, showed that which his looks never would have done, that he was a Friar. Beneath his bushy black brows danced a pair of little grey eyes that could not stand still for very drollery of humour.

His legs were stretched wide apart, and betwixt his knees he held a great pasty compounded of juicy meats of diverse kinds made savoury with tender young onions being mingled with a good rich gravy. In his right fist he held a great piece of brown crust at which he munched steadily, and every now and then he thrust his left hand into the pie and drew it forth full of meat; anon he would take a mighty pull at a great bottle of Malmsey that lay beside him.

'By my faith,' quoth Robin to himself, 'I do verily believe that this is the merriest feast, the merriest wight, the merriest place, and the merriest sight in all merry England.'

from Howard Pyle's *Robin Hood*

If a national referendum were taken on the subject of picnic food, there is little doubt that quiches, pizzas and pies would win

96

without much effort. There seems to be a variety to suit every taste and their popularity continues all year round. They present no packing problems and can, in various sizes, be tucked into a basket, a box or a pocket.

Quiches, Pizzas, Pies Tips

***** As wholewheat and wheatmeal pastry is slightly difficult to handle when cold, roll it out first on a sheet of greaseproof paper (this will keep it from sticking). Use to line flan or tartlet tins and then chill for 30 minutes before baking.

***** When baking a quiche or flan case for a picnic, be sure to bake it blind first (for 12–15 minutes) so that the filling doesn't make it soggy.

***** Always take quiches out of their tins to cool (otherwise they will have a shiny, marzipan-like finish on the base).

***** *To pack hot quiche:* take straight from the oven, slide the quiche on to a loose flan base (if using a flan ring) or simply cover the flan tin with foil and pack in an insulated bag.

***** *To pack cold quiche:* slide the quiche from the cooling rack on to a plate or loose flan base. Cover with foil or cling film and pack on the top layer of the basket.

***** If space is a problem, pack mini-pizzas in a tall, cylindrical biscuit tin, separating each one with a double thickness of greaseproof paper or foil. When ready to serve, slide the pizzas gently on to a plate and remove the papers. (This is also a good way of storing the pizzas and if the tin is put into the refrigerator they will stay fresh for several days.)

Pastry

PLAIN SHORTCRUST PASTRY

8oz (225g) plain flour   2oz (50g) butter
large pinch of salt   2oz (50g) lard or margarine
                    4 tablespoons iced water

Sift the flour and salt into a large mixing bowl. Cut the butter and lard into the flour with two knives, then rub in with finger-tips until the mixture resembles breadcrumbs. Then sprinkle the iced water over the dry mixture and mix with a fork or knife until it leaves the sides of the bowl clean. Shape into a ball, knead lightly until smooth and then put into a polythene bag or wrap in cling film. Chill for 30 minutes before using. Then take out and leave at room temperature for 5 minutes before rolling.

RICH SHORTCRUST PASTRY

8oz (225g) plain flour   *or:* 12oz (350g) plain flour
large pinch of salt   large pinch of salt
4oz (100g) butter   6oz (175g) butter
2oz (50g) lard   2oz (50g) lard
1 standard egg yolk   2 standard egg yolks
3–4 tablespoons iced water   4–6 tablespoons iced water

Sift the flour and salt into a large mixing bowl. Cut the butter and lard in with two knives, then rub in lightly with fingertips until the mixture resembles breadcrumbs. Mix the egg yolks with the water and pour over the dry mixture. Mix quickly with a fork or knife until it leaves the sides of the bowl clean. Shape into a ball, knead lightly until smooth, then wrap in cling film or a polythene bag. Chill for 30 minutes before using. Leave at room temperature for 5 minutes before rolling.

WHOLEWHEAT PASTRY

8oz (225g) self-raising whole- 2oz (50g) butter
   wheat flour 2oz (50g) lard
large pinch of salt 4–6 tablespoons iced water

Sift the flour and salt into a large mixing bowl, then tip in the bran that remains in the sieve. Cut the butter and lard into the flour with two knives, then rub in lightly with fingertips until it resembles breadcrumbs. Add the iced water and mix quickly with a fork or knife until it leaves the sides of the bowl clean. Shape into a ball and knead lightly until smooth. Roll out and use to line flan or tartlet tins. Then chill for 30 minutes before baking.

WHEATMEAL PASTRY

4oz (100g) plain flour 2oz (50g) butter
4oz (100g) wholewheat flour 2oz (50g) lard
large pinch of salt 4–6 tablespoons iced water

Sift the flours and salt into a large mixing bowl, then tip in the bran that remains in the sieve. Cut the butter and lard in with two knives, then rub in lightly with fingertips until the mixture resembles breadcrumbs. Add the iced water and mix in quickly with a fork or knife until it leaves the sides of the bowl clean. Shape into a ball and knead lightly until smooth. Roll out and use to line flan or tartlet tins. Then chill for 30 minutes before baking.

HOT WATER PASTRY

12oz (350g) plain flour large pinch of pepper
1 teaspoon salt 5oz (150g) lard
        5oz (150ml) milk or water

Sift the flour, salt and pepper into a large mixing bowl, then put in warm place. Dissolve the lard in the milk or water and bring to the boil. Make a well in the centre of the flour, tip in the boiling liquid and mix quickly with a wooden spoon. Turn out on to a lightly floured counter and knead until smooth. Then roll out or shape according to the recipe used.

PIZZA DOUGH

8oz (225g) plain flour
1 level teaspoon salt
¼oz (7g) fresh yeast or
  1 teaspoon dried yeast plus

¼ teaspoon sugar
5oz (150ml) warm water
1 dessertspoon oil

Loose base of a 9″ (23cm) flan tin, well greased

Dissolve the fresh yeast in the warm water. If using dried yeast, put it in a small bowl with the sugar and mix with 5oz (150ml) hand-hot water. Leave in a warm place for about 15 minutes or until frothy.

Sift the flour and salt into a large mixing bowl. Make a well in the centre and mix in the yeast liquid and the oil, using a wooden spoon. Stir until the dough leaves the sides of the bowl clean. Then turn out on to a well-floured counter and knead until smooth and no longer sticky (this takes about 5 minutes). Then put back into the mixing bowl and cover with cling film or a greased polythene bag. Leave until doubled in size (when the dough is pressed with a floured finger, it should spring back).

Turn out on to a lightly floured counter and pummel with knuckles to knock out any large air bubbles, then knead back into shape. Roll or press with fingers into a circle large and flat enough to cover the 9″ (23cm) base, turning the edges up slightly.

Brush lightly with oil, then cover with pizza sauce (see pages 108–111 for recipes) and bake as directed.

QUICK PIZZA DOUGH

8oz (225g) self-raising flour   2oz (50g) butter
½ teaspoon salt   5oz (150ml) milk

Baking tray or loose base of an 8″ (20cm) or 9″ (23cm) flan tin, well greased

Sift the flour and salt together into a large mixing bowl. Rub in the butter until the mixture resembles breadcrumbs, then pour in the milk and blend in with a fork or round-topped knife.

Turn the dough out on to a lightly floured counter and knead gently for half a minute until smooth. Roll out until ¼″/·50cm thick. Then press with fingers into one large round or small individual rounds (these can be made by cutting round the edge of an inverted saucer or teacup). Press down very flat with your fingers and turn the edges up slightly to keep the sauce from escaping.

Spread the dough with a small amount of soft butter, then cover with cheese and sauce (see recipe for Mini Pizzas). Bake as directed.

Quiches

QUICHE LORRAINE

6oz (175g) rich shortcrust   3 large eggs
   pastry   5oz (150ml) single cream
1oz (25g) butter   4oz (100g) Gruyère cheese,
1 large onion   grated
6oz (175g) bacon rashers   pinch of dry mustard
       salt and pepper

8″ (20cm) flan ring or tin
Preheat oven to 375°F / Gas Mark 5 / 190°C.

101

Roll out the pastry and use to line the flan tin. Prick the base lightly with a fork, then cover base and sides with a circle of greaseproof paper. Fill with baking beans and bake in the centre of the oven for 10 minutes. Remove the paper and beans and cook for a further 5 minutes. Put to one side.

Remove the rind, then cut the bacon into small pieces. Chop the onion finely and sauté both in the butter. Cook over moderate heat until the onion is golden brown.

Beat the eggs with the cream and mustard, then add salt and pepper to taste. Mix in half the grated cheese with the cooked onion and bacon. Pour into the pastry case and sprinkle with the remaining cheese.

Bake at the same temperature (as above) for 20–25 minutes or until set and lightly browned. Remove from the tin and cool on a wire rack. Then slide on to a plate or loose flan base, cover with cling film and pack. Or, take straight from the oven, cover with foil and pack in an insulated bag.

Serves 4–6

SPRING ONION AND CRESS QUICHE

This is particularly attractive (and delicious) if made in tartlet tins, using wholewheat or wheatmeal pastry.

6oz (175g) wholewheat or
 plain shortcrust pastry
½oz (15g) butter
14 spring onions
1 bunch of watercress

3 large eggs
5oz (150ml) single cream or
 rich milk (or milk and cream
 mixed)
4oz (100g) cheddar cheese
salt and pepper

Tartlet tins or an 8″ (20cm) flan ring or tin
Preheat oven to 375°F / Gas Mark 5 / 190°C.

Line the flan ring (or tartlet tins) with pastry, prick the base lightly with a fork and cover the base and sides with a circle of greaseproof paper. Fill with baking beans and bake for about 10 minutes. Remove the paper and beans and bake for a further 5 minutes. Put to one side.

Melt the butter in a frying pan and add the spring onions, washed and sliced into small pieces. Wash and chop the watercress finely and add to the onions when they are soft but not coloured. Toss well in the butter and cook over gentle heat for 5 minutes. Then draw off the heat.

Beat the eggs, then blend in the cream. Season to taste with salt and pepper. Grate the cheese and add half to the egg mixture, reserving the rest. Cover the base of the flan with the onion and cress mixture (or divide evenly between the tartlets), then pour over the egg mixture and top with the remaining cheese.

Bake in the centre of the oven for 25 minutes (or on the second shelf from the top of the oven for 20–25 minutes, if tartlets) or until set. Cover with foil and pack in an insulated bag or leave to cool on a wire rack. Then slide on to a loose flan base or put back into the flan or tartlet tins. Cover with foil or cling film and pack.

Serves 4–6

QUICHE PAYSANNE

6oz (175g) wholewheat or
   shortcrust pastry
1½oz (40g) butter
4oz (100g) mushrooms
4 gammon rashers
1 medium onion
1 small cooked potato

2 large eggs
¼ pint (150ml) single cream
2oz (50g) cheddar cheese,
   grated
salt and black pepper
chopped parsley or herbs (fresh
   or dried)

8″ (20cm) flan ring, tin or dish (or tartlet tins)
Preheat oven to 375°F / Gas Mark 5 / 190°C.
Roll out the pastry to a circle just slightly larger than the flan

tin. Fit carefully into the tin, trim off any surplus and prick the base lightly with a fork. Then cover the base and sides with a circle of crumpled greaseproof paper and fill with baking beans. Bake in the centre of the oven for 15 minutes, removing the paper and beans for the last 5 minutes. Then put to one side.

Melt 1oz (25g) of butter in a large frying pan. Slice the onion thinly and chop the gammon rashers (remove the rind first) into small pieces. Sauté both in the butter until the onion is soft and transparent. Wash the mushrooms and cut into small dice. Add to the pan and cook for about 5 minutes or until they have darkened in colour. Add the remaining butter and the potato, sliced thinly. Cook for a further 10 minutes, shaking the pan occasionally to keep the vegetables from sticking. Then sprinkle generously with salt and pepper.

Beat the eggs lightly, then blend in the cream. Season well with salt and freshly ground black pepper. Spread the vegetable mixture evenly over the base of the flan case. Cover with the beaten eggs and cream, then top with the grated cheese and chopped parsley (or herbs). Bake in the centre of a preheated oven for about 25 minutes or until set. Then take out, remove from the tin and leave to cool on a wire rack. When ready to pack, slide on to a plate or loose flan base and cover with cling film or foil. Or, take straight from the oven, cover with foil and pack in an insulated bag.

Serves 4–6

ASPARAGUS QUICHE

6oz (175g) shortcrust pastry*
1 small onion or 8 spring
  onions
½oz (15g) butter
1 (12oz/340g) tin of asparagus

3oz (75g) Gruyère or cheddar
  cheese, grated
3 large eggs
¼ pint (150ml) rich milk or
  single cream

¼ teaspoon French mustard

* Avoid using wholewheat or wheatmeal pastry as it tends to overwhelm the subtle flavour of the asparagus.

8" (20cm) flan ring or tin or tartlet tins
Preheat oven to 375°F / Gas Mark 5 / 190°C.

Roll out the pastry and use to line the flan tin. Prick the base
lightly with a fork and cover the base and sides with a large
circle of greaseproof paper. Fill with baking beans and bake for
about 10 minutes. Then remove the paper and beans and bake
for a further 5 minutes.

Melt the butter in a frying pan and cook the onion, finely
chopped, until soft and transparent. Put into a small mixing bowl
with the eggs, cream and mustard, and beat until light and
frothy. Add salt and pepper to taste.

Put a sprinkling of grated cheese over the bottom of the pastry
case and arrange the asparagus pinwheel fashion on top. Cover
with the egg mixture and top with the remaining cheese. Bake in
the centre of the oven for 25 minutes (if tartlets, on the second
shelf from the top for 20 minutes) or until lightly browned. Cool
on a wire rack, then slide on to a plate or loose flan base, cover
with foil or cling film and pack. (If packing straight away, see
the section on Keeping Food Hot.)

Serves 4–6

QUICHE PROVENCALE

8oz (225g) rich shortcrust or wheatmeal pastry
1 small onion
4oz (100g) mushrooms
1oz (25g) butter
1 medium courgette
1 (14oz/398ml) tin of tomatoes or 4 large ripe tomatoes

pinch of dried rosemary or basil
1 teaspoon sugar
½ teaspoon dried mixed herbs
3 eggs
¼ pint (150ml) single cream
3oz (75g) cheddar cheese, grated

9" (23cm) flan tin or dish, or tartlet tins
Preheat oven to 375°F / Gas Mark 5 / 190°C.

Chop the onion finely, then wipe the mushrooms and cut into
very small pieces. Sauté both in the butter until soft, stirring
occasionally.

Wipe the courgette with kitchen paper and chop into small dice. Then add to the pan with the tomatoes (chopped) and their juice. Add the dried rosemary, sugar and mixed herbs. Mix well and leave to cook over gentle heat until all the ingredients are soft and cooked through.

In the meantime, line the flan dish or tartlet tins with pastry and bake blind in a preheated oven for about 15 minutes (12 minutes for tartlets). Remove the paper and baking beans for the last 5 minutes of cooking. Take out of the oven and sprinkle the base of the flan evenly with half the grated cheese. Then cover with the courgette mixture.

Lightly beat the eggs, stir in the cream and season to taste with salt and pepper. Pour over the filling and top with the remaining cheese. Bake at the same temperature as above for 25 minutes (20 minutes for tartlets) or until set. Remove from the tin(s) and cool on a wire rack. Then slide on to a plate or loose flan base (or, if tartlets, put back in the tins), cover with cling film and pack. Or, take straight from the oven, cover with foil and pack in an insulated bag.

Serves 4–6

PRAWN AND CREAM CHEESE QUICHE

6oz (175g) rich shortcrust pastry
4oz (100g) prawns
3oz (75g) cream cheese
3 large eggs

5oz (150ml) double or single cream
2oz (50g) cheddar cheese, grated
sprinkling of dried parsley

salt and pepper to taste

8″ (20cm) flan ring or tin
Preheat oven to 375°F / Gas Mark 5 / 190°C.

Line the flan tin with pastry, prick the base lightly with a fork and cover the base and sides with a circle of greaseproof paper. Fill with baking beans and bake for 10 minutes. Then remove the beans and paper and bake for a further 5 minutes. Put to one side until the filling is ready.

Soften the cream cheese in a bowl and gradually blend in the cream. Beat the eggs lightly and mix in. Then stir in the prawns. Season to taste with salt and pepper.

Fill the pastry case with the egg and prawn mixture. Sprinkle with the grated cheese and chopped fresh or dried parsley. Bake in the centre of the oven for about 25 minutes or until set. Cover with foil and pack in an insulated bag or in any of the ways suggested in the section on Keeping Food Hot. To serve cold: cool on a wire rack, then slide on to a loose flan base, cover with foil or cling film and pack.

Serves 4–6

PISSALADIERE

6oz (175g) rich shortcrust pastry	1 (14oz/398ml) tin of tomatoes
1 (2oz/50g) tin anchovy fillets	1½ teaspoons sugar
small amount of milk	½ teaspoon each of dried marjoram, basil and oregano (or
1 large green pepper	1½ teaspoons of dried mixed
1 large onion	herbs)

Parmesan cheese

Tartlet tins or 8″ (20cm) flan ring or tin
Preheat oven to 375°F / Gas Mark 5 / 190°C.

Put the anchovy fillets on a small saucer, cover with milk and leave for about 15 minutes. Then drain.

Line the tartlet tins (or flan tin) with pastry, prick the base with a fork and cover the base and sides with a circle of greaseproof paper. Fill with baking beans and bake on the second shelf from the top of the oven (or centre for flan) for about 10 minutes. Remove the paper and beans and cook for a further 5 minutes. Put to one side.

Slice the onion and pepper into thin strips. Melt the butter in a large frying pan and, when foaming, add the onion and pepper.

Toss well in the butter and leave to cook over moderate heat until the onions are golden brown. Add the tomatoes, sugar, herbs and a good sprinkling of salt and black pepper. Continue cooking for 10–15 minutes more until the mixture is slightly thickened (but not dry).

Divide the tomato mixture amongst the pastry cases and top each one with a crisscross of anchovy fillets and a sprinkling of Parmesan cheese. Bake on the second shelf from the top of the oven for 15–20 minutes. (Bake the flan in the centre of the oven for 20–25 minutes.)

Leave to cool slightly, then remove from the tins. Cool on a wire rack. Put in a tin or plastic container and pack. (Or take straight from the oven, cover with foil and pack in an insulated bag.)

Serves 4–6

Pizzas

TRADITIONAL PIZZA

8oz (225g) pizza dough
1oz (25g) butter
1 medium onion
1 (14oz/400g) tin tomatoes
½ teaspoon sugar
½ teaspoon each of dried basil, oregano and marjoram (or

1½ teaspoons dried mixed herbs)
salt and black pepper
6oz (175g) mozarella or cheddar cheese
olives to decorate
olive or vegetable oil

Grease a 9″ (23cm) loose base from flan or cake tin (or a baking tray).

Prepare the pizza dough, following the recipe given on page 100. Leave to rise, then begin the sauce.

Melt the butter in a large frying pan and add the onion,

chopped finely. Cook until soft and transparent, then stir in the tomatoes (chopped into small pieces) with their juice. Add the sugar, herbs and a good sprinkling of salt and black pepper. Cook over moderate heat until slightly thick but not dry. Check the seasoning and put to one side.

When the dough has doubled in size, turn out on to a lightly floured counter and pummel with knuckles to knock out any large air bubbles. Then roll or press with fingers into a large round. Lift on to greased flan base and press very flat.

Slice the cheese thinly and use two-thirds of it to cover the base of the pizza (brush lightly with olive or vegetable oil first). Then cover with the tomato sauce. Cut the remaining cheese into thin strips and arrange pinwheel fashion on top of the pizza. Decorate with black olives. Bake in the centre of a preheated oven (425°F / Gas Mark 7 / 220°C) for 20–30 minutes. Cover with foil and pack in an insulated bag. Or leave to cool and cover with foil just before packing.

Serves 8

PIZZA QUATRO STAGIONE

8oz (225g) pizza dough
1oz (25g) butter
1 medium onion
2oz (50g) cooked ham
   (2 slices)
4oz (100g) fresh mushrooms
½ large green pepper
1 small tin (5oz/150g) tomato
   purée

3 tablespoons water
2 teaspoons mixed dried herbs
1 teaspoon sugar
squeeze of lemon juice
salt and pepper
4oz (100g) mozarella or
   cheddar cheese
Parmesan cheese
small amount of vegetable oil

Grease a 9" (23cm) loose base from a flan or cake tin or a baking tray.
Prepare the pizza dough, following the recipe given on page 100. Leave to rise, then begin the sauce.

Melt the butter in a large frying pan. Slice the onion and cook quickly for about 10 minutes until soft and transparent. Then lift with a fish slice out of the frying pan and put to one side. Chop the ham into small dice and cook in the butter for 5 minutes, then remove from the pan. Blanch the green pepper in boiling water for a minute and slice into thin strips. Sauté (add more butter if necessary) until soft, then put on to a plate. Wipe and slice the mushrooms thinly. Cook very quickly in the frying pan until just soft and take off the heat.

Take the risen pizza dough and pummel with knuckles on a lightly floured counter to knock out any large air bubbles. Then roll or press out with fingers into a very flat round. Lift on to greased flan base and turn the edges up slightly to keep the sauce from escaping. Brush the surface lightly with oil. Slice the cheese thinly and use to cover the pizza base. Then mix the tomato purée, sugar, mixed herbs, water, lemon juice, salt and pepper in a small bowl. Spread evenly over the cheese. With a knife, mark the top into 4 equal triangles and fill each with a different ingredient: ham, onions, pepper or mushrooms, making sure that the lines between them are kept distinct. Sprinkle with a small amount of Parmesan cheese.

Bake in the centre of a hot oven (425°F/Gas Mark 7/220°C) for about 20–30 minutes. Take out, cover with foil and pack immediately in an insulated bag (or leave to cool and cover with foil just before packing).

Serves 8

PIZZA NAPOLETANA

8oz (225g) pizza dough
1 (2oz/50g) tin anchovy fillets
2–3 tablespoons milk
1 medium onion
1oz (25g) butter or
   2–3 tablespoons vegetable
   oil
1 (14oz/398g) tin of tomatoes

1 teaspoon sugar
½ teaspoon each of oregano,
   basil and marjoram, or 1½
   teaspoons mixed herbs
salt and pepper
4oz–6oz (100g–175g) cheddar
   or mozarella cheese
8–10 black olives
soft butter or vegetable oil

110

9″ (23cm) loose base from a flan or cake tin (or a baking tray),
well greased

Make up the pizza dough, following the recipe given on page 100.
Leave in a warm place to rise, then prepare the pizza sauce.

First put the anchovies on a saucer and cover with milk (this
takes away some of the saltiness), then leave until needed. Peel
the onion and chop finely. Sauté in the butter or oil until very
soft and just coloured. Mash the tomatoes, then add to the pan
with the sugar, herbs and a sprinkling of salt and pepper. Cook
over moderate heat for about 20 minutes, stirring from time to
time to prevent sticking, until the mixture is quite thick.

When the pizza dough has doubled in size, turn out on to a
lightly floured counter and pummel with knuckles to knock out
any large air bubbles. Then knead back into shape again and
with a rolling pin, or hands, press into a flat circle to fit the flan
or cake tin base (the pizza should be baked only on the base
and not in the tin itself) which has been greased well. Press the
dough down firmly with fingers, then spread with a small amount
of soft butter or brush lightly with vegetable oil. Slice the
cheddar or mozarella thinly and cover the dough with it, reserving several slices for the top. Check the sauce for seasoning,
then spread it evenly over the cheese. Pour the milk off the
anchovies and drain on kitchen paper. Arrange pinwheel fashion
on top of the pizza. Put 1 black olive in the centre and the others
round the edge. Grate the remaining cheese and sprinkle in the
triangles formed by the anchovies. Bake in the centre of a hot
oven (425°F / Gas Mark 7 / 220°C) for 20–30 minutes or until
the crust is a light golden brown. Leave to cool, then cover with
foil and pack. Or take straight from the oven, cover with foil and
pack in an insulated bag.

Serves 8

MINI PIZZAS (Quick)

I doubt if the Italians would approve of these but they are marvellous for last-minute picnics.

8oz (225g) quick pizza dough
1oz (25g) soft butter
1 small tin (5oz/150g) tomato purée
2 tablespoons tomato ketchup
2 tablespoons Parmesan cheese

2 tablespoons water
1 tablespoon sugar
2 teaspoons dried mixed herbs
1 teaspoon dried onion flakes
4oz (100g) cheddar or mozarella cheese

Grease a large baking tray.
Preheat oven to 450°F / Gas Mark 8 / 230°C.

Make up the pizza dough, following the recipe given on page 101. Roll out until ¼" (·50cm) thick. Then make small pizza bases by cutting round the edge of an inverted saucer or teacup (you can make these bases as big or as small as you like). Lift on to the greased tray and press each circle down very flat with your fingers, turning the edges up slightly to keep the sauce from escaping. Spread each one with a small amount of soft butter.

Put the tomato purée, tomato ketchup, half the Parmesan cheese, water, sugar, mixed herbs and onion flakes in a bowl and mix together well. Slice the cheese thinly and cut to fit each pizza base. Press the cheese slightly into the dough, then cover with the tomato sauce. Sprinkle with the remaining Parmesan cheese. Bake just above the centre of a preheated oven for about 20 minutes. Cool on a wire rack, then slide into a tin or on to a plate, cover with foil and pack. Or take straight from the oven, put into a biscuit tin (separating the pizza layers with foil) or large aluminium container and pack in an insulated bag.

Makes 6–10 mini pizzas

Pies

VEAL AND HAM PIE

10oz (275g) rich or plain shortcrust pastry
1½lb (675g) pie veal
8oz (225g) cooked ham
½ small onion
grated rind of ½ lemon
1 tablespoon chopped fresh or
dried parsley
1½ teaspoons gelatine

8oz (225ml) well-seasoned
chicken stock (or ½ chicken
stock cube dissolved in 8oz/
225ml boiling water)
salt and freshly ground black
pepper
3 large hard-boiled eggs
beaten egg to glaze

8½″ (21·5cm) pie plate

Make up the pastry (see pp. 98–9 for recipes) and chill until the
filling is ready or thaw frozen shortcrust.

Cut the veal and ham into small pieces and put into a large
mixing bowl. Chop the onion finely and add with 2oz (50ml) of
the chicken stock, lemon rind, parsley and a sprinkling of salt
and black pepper. Mix well, then leave to soak until all the
chicken stock has been absorbed (stir occasionally so that it
doesn't sit at the bottom of the bowl). Boil the eggs until hard,
put into a bowl of cold water, then remove the shells.

Roll out two-thirds of the pastry thinly and use to line the pie
plate. Trim the edges, then dampen slightly with water. Put in
a layer of the veal and ham mixture. Slice the eggs in half
lengthwise and place flat side down in a circle on top of the
meat. Cover with the remaining veal and ham and mound it up
slightly in the centre to give a domed effect. Roll out the pastry
that is left and place it on top. Trim off any surplus, pinch the
edges together, knock up and flute. Decorate with any pastry
trimmings, then cut a small hole in the top to let the steam
escape. Brush with beaten egg and bake in the centre of a preheated oven (400°F / Gas Mark 6 / 200°C) for 1¼ hours (if the

top is getting too brown, cover loosely with foil). Take out and cool completely.

Put the remaining chicken stock into a small cup and sprinkle 1½ teaspoons of gelatine on top. Let it soak for 5 minutes then dissolve completely over hot water. Leave until just beginning to set, then pour through the hole in the pastry lid (tipping the plate slightly so that the stock is evenly distributed) when the pie is quite cold. Cover with a loose 'hood' of foil and pack.

Serves 6–8

RAISED CHICKEN AND MUSHROOM PIE

12oz (350g) rich or plain short-crust pastry
1 (4lb/2kg) chicken with giblets
½ pint (275ml) chicken stock (fresh or made with a stock cube)

1½oz (40g) soft butter
1 large onion
1lb (450g) button mushrooms
1 large bunch of fresh parsley
salt and freshly ground black pepper

8″ (20cm) spring-form cake tin
Preheat oven to 375°F / Gas Mark 5 / 190°C.

Wipe the chicken dry, then rub with ½oz (40g) soft butter and put a large knob inside the neck cavity. Put in a roasting tin with the giblets and pour over the chicken stock. Bake in a pre-heated oven for an hour or until done, basting occasionally with the pan juices. Then pour the liquid into a jug and leave the chicken to cool.

When cool enough to handle, remove the skin, take off all the chicken flesh and cut into bite-size pieces. Put into a mixing bowl, season well, and toss in 5oz (150ml) of the chicken stock. (Put the remaining stock into the refrigerator.) Leave until all the liquid has been absorbed. Melt the butter that is left and sauté the onion (finely chopped) until soft and transparent. Wipe

114

the mushrooms and cut into small dice. Add to the onion and cook for several minutes until just soft. Rinse the parsley, blanch for several seconds in boiling water and refresh by rinsing under cold water. Chop finely and put to one side.

Roll out two-thirds of the pastry and use to line the base and sides of the tin. Then fill with a layer of chicken, then one of mushroom and onion, parsley and another of chicken. Roll out the remaining pastry, dampen the edges and cover the pie. Pinch together, knock up and flute the edges. Cut a small hole in the top to let the steam escape. Use any pastry trimmings to decorate the top, then brush with beaten egg. Bake in the centre of a pre-heated oven (400°F / Gas Mark 6 / 200°C) for 40 minutes or until golden brown. Leave to cool, then remove the spring-form band and brush the sides of the pie with beaten egg. Cover the top loosely with foil and return to the oven for a further 15–20 minutes or until the sides are golden. Cool completely. Take the jellied stock out of the refrigerator, skim off the fat and dissolve the stock over gentle heat. Leave in a cool place until just beginning to thicken again, then carefully pour through the hole in the pastry lid, tipping the pie slightly as you do it so that the stock is well distributed. Chill for at least an hour. When ready to pack, leave the pie on its tin base and cover loosely with foil.

Serves 8–10

INDIVIDUAL MEAT PIES

12oz (350g) shortcrust pastry
½oz (15g) butter
½ large onion
5oz (150g) carrots
1 clove garlic
½ pint (275ml) beef stock (fresh or made with a stock cube)

¾lb (350g) lean minced beef
2 large ripe tomatoes
large pinch of parsley
large pinch of dried mixed herbs
salt and black pepper
beaten egg to glaze

Patty or small pie tins

Melt the butter in a large saucepan and add the onion, chopped finely. Peel the carrots and cut into very small dice. Put in the saucepan, toss well in the butter and sauté until the onion is soft but not coloured. Crush the garlic in a small amount of salt, then add to the pan with the minced beef and the stock. Add a good sprinkling of salt and pepper, mix well and bring to the boil. Then reduce the heat and simmer uncovered for 20 minutes. Stir in the chopped tomatoes and cook for 10–20 minutes more, or until almost all the liquid has evaporated but the meat is still moist. Take off the heat and leave to cool.

Roll out two-thirds of the pastry and cut out circles to line the patty tins. Fit these into the tins and trim off any surplus. Then fill each one generously with the meat mixture and dampen the edges lightly with water. Roll out the remaining pastry, then cut out lids for the pies. Place on top, pinch the edges together and cut several slits to let the steam escape. Brush with beaten egg and bake in the centre of a preheated oven (400°F/Gas Mark 6/ 200°C) for 40 minutes or until golden brown. Leave in the tins for several minutes, then take out carefully and cool on a wire rack (or wrap in foil and pack in an insulated bag).

Makes 12 small meat pies

COUNTRY CHICKEN PIES

4oz (100g) rich shortcrust or flaky pastry
4oz (100g) carrots
1¼ pints (700ml) well-seasoned chicken stock
8oz (225g) peas (fresh or frozen)
1oz (25g) butter
2 level tablespoons flour
4 large cooked chicken breasts
salt and pepper

4 large or 6 small ramekin dishes

Pare the carrots, slice into thin julienne strips and chop into small dice. Put ½ pint (275ml) of the chicken stock into a saucepan and bring to the boil. Add the carrots and a good sprinkling of salt. Bring back to the boil, then simmer gently for 5 minutes or until almost tender. Add the peas and cook for another 5 minutes. Drain the liquid into a jug and put the vegetables to one side.

Melt the butter in a large saucepan, stir in the flour and cook for 1 minute. Take off the heat and gradually stir in ½ pint (275ml) chicken stock. Cook over moderate heat, stirring constantly, until thickened. Then pour in the remaining stock and the vegetable juices. Cook over gentle heat for another 5–10 minutes* then stir in the cooked vegetables and season to taste with salt and pepper. Remove the skin and chop the chicken into bite-size pieces. Add to the sauce, then leave to cool slightly.

Roll out the pastry and cut out circles just slightly larger than the ramekins. Fill the dishes to the top with the chicken mixture. Dampen the edges of the pastry, then cover each dish with a lid. Press firmly around the sides to seal, then knock up and flute the edges. Brush lightly with beaten egg and cut several small slits in the top to let the steam escape. Put on a baking tray and bake in a preheated oven (375°F / Gas Mark 5 / 190°C) for 35–40 minutes or until golden brown. Take out, cover with foil and pack in an insulated bag. Or leave to cool, then cover and pack.

Makes 4–6 pies

* The sauce will be very thin but don't be alarmed; this keeps it from clotting and ensures a juicy filling when the pies are served cold.

Recipes for the following can be found in other parts of the book: Grouse Pie (p. 222), Veal and Ham II (p. 215).

7

MEAT, CHICKEN AND FISH DISHES

. . . Then cold meat – or cold fish – need not call up
visions of a distasteful-looking joint, with icicles of cold,
unappetising fat. Cut it up! Cut it up, and surround it
with lettuce, or cover it with sliced beetroot, or mix it up
with salad in a bowl, and no one will grumble and most
be pleased.

from *Homely Hints* by Monsieur Alphonse (1902)

Comparing the difference in cost between a late-Victorian picnic
and one given today, it is easy to see why meat and fish dishes,
which featured so prominently then, have fallen from favour.
(In a turn-of-the-century edition of Mrs Beeton, the price of
3lb of salmon is quoted as 4s 6d; 2 chickens, 5s; 6lb of cold
beef, 5s, and a quarter of lamb as 9s!)

For this reason the recipes in this chapter have been kept as
modest as possible. With several exceptions (intended for special
picnics), they shouldn't put undue strain on the purse-strings.

Meat, Chicken and Fish Tips

****** When buying chicken for a picnic, choose thigh or leg
joints as they are easy to eat with fingers. Or buy a whole
chicken and cut into manageable portions, after roasting, with
poultry shears or kitchen scissors.

****** The wide-necked Thermos flasks can be used very successfully for transporting and serving hot food so that the picnic menu no longer needs to be restricted to cold meat and fish dishes. To prepare the Thermos, see the introductory section on Keeping Food Hot.

****** Chicken, meat and fish can all be precooked in foil for part of their cooking time in the oven and then finished off (in the same piece of foil) on a barbecue. For packing, however, it's best to wrap the meat in a second piece of heavy foil to prevent leakage.

****** When baking meat or fish 'en papillote', leave to cool in the foil. This will keep it moist and retain all the juices. Check for tears in the foil before packing, and if even slightly damp, wrap in another piece of foil.

****** Though Chinese and Japanese food may seem like odd choices for a picnic, they travel extremely well in aluminium-foil containers with lids. The steamy atmosphere created when the hot container is packed in a polythene bag (see the introductory section on Keeping Food Hot) is one which they thrive on.

SPICEY MEAT LOAF

6 tablespoons tomato pickle or chilli sauce
1 tablespoon Worcestershire sauce
large pinch sugar
1 teaspoon lemon juice
1 teaspoon salt
freshly ground black pepper
1½lb (675g) lean minced beef
1 large slice wholemeal bread
1 large egg

1½lb (675g) loaf tin
Line a small baking tray with foil.
Preheat oven to 350°F / Gas Mark 4 / 180°C.

119

Put the tomato pickle, Worcestershire sauce, sugar, lemon juice, salt and pepper into a bowl and mix well.

In another bowl, put the minced meat and the bread, crumbled into small pieces (coarse breadcrumbs). Beat the egg lightly and add to the meat with two-thirds of the sauce. Blend well with a fork or wooden spoon until the mixture binds together. Then press into the loaf tin, cover with foil and cook in the centre of the oven for 30 minutes. Remove the foil, reverse the loaf on to the prepared tray and coat with the remaining sauce. Bake for a further 30 minutes, basting from time to time. Cool on a wire rack (to drain excess grease). Then wrap in foil and keep in a cool place until needed. Or take straight from the oven, wrap in a double layer of foil and pack in an insulated bag.

Serves 6–8

MEAT LOAF EN CROUTE

12oz (350g) puff pastry (frozen or home-made)
2lb (1kg) lean minced beef
1oz (25g) butter
1 large onion
8oz (225g) button mushrooms

1 teaspoon salt
¼ teaspoon black pepper
2 teaspoons dried mixed herbs
2 slices wholemeal bread
1 large egg
6oz (175g) smooth pâté

2lb (9"/23cm) loaf tin
Preheat oven to 350°F / Gas Mark 4 / 180°C.

Chop the onion and mushrooms very finely, then sauté in the butter until soft.

Put the minced beef into a large mixing bowl and blend in half the onion/mushroom mixture, salt, black pepper and dried herbs. Then crumble the bread into very small pieces and mix in. Beat the egg lightly, then use to bind the mixture together. Press into the loaf tin, cover with foil and bake in the centre of the oven for 30 minutes. Carefully turn out on to a wire rack and leave to cool.

Roll out the puff pastry thinly to a rectangle about 4″ (10cm) longer than the meat loaf and three times its width. Mix the remaining onion/mushroom mixture with the pâté and spread evenly over the pastry, leaving a 1″ (2·5cm) border around the edges. Put the cooled loaf, bottom side up, in the centre of the pastry. Dampen the edges, bring the sides up and fold over the loaf. Pinch the edges together. Do the same at the ends, just as you would wrap a parcel. Turn over, decorate the top with pastry trimmings, and make several slits to allow the steam to escape. Brush with beaten egg and place on a baking tray. Bake in the centre of a preheated oven (425°F / Gas Mark 7 / 220°C) for 40 minutes or until golden brown. Take from the oven, leave to cool, then wrap in foil. Or take straight from the oven, wrap in foil and pack in an insulated bag.

Serves 8–10

TUNA LOAF

2 (7oz/200g) tins of tuna
4 hard-boiled eggs
8oz (225g) cooked peas
1 teaspoon lemon juice
12 water biscuits

1 tablespoon chopped parsley
  (fresh or dried)
salt and black pepper
1oz (25g) butter
2 level tablespoons flour
½ pint (275ml) milk

Line a 1lb (450g) loaf tin with foil.
Preheat oven to 350°F / Gas Mark 4 / 180°C.

Peel the eggs and chop finely. Drain the tuna well on absorbent kitchen paper and put into a medium bowl. Flake with a fork, then add the chopped eggs, lemon juice, green peas, chopped parsley, salt (only a pinch as the tuna is salty) and freshly ground black pepper. Crumble the water biscuits into small pieces and mix in.

Melt the butter in a small saucepan, take off the heat and stir in the flour. Cook for 1 minute then gradually blend in the milk (off the heat). Cook over moderate heat until thick, stirring all the time. Add salt and pepper to taste, then fold into the tuna mixture. When well blended, turn the mixture into the lined tin. Cover with foil and bake in the centre of the oven for 30 minutes. Cool in the tin, then lift out carefully. Wrap in another piece of foil and pack. Or reverse out on to a plate and cover with foil or cling film. Serve sliced with salad.

Serves 6–8

VIRGINIA BAKED HAM LOAF

¾lb (350g) ground cooked ham
¾lb (350g) ground pork
1 small onion

2 teaspoons French mustard
2oz (50g) fresh breadcrumbs
1 egg, beaten
7oz (200ml) milk

salt and pepper

Glaze:
3oz (75g) butter, at room temperature
3oz (75g) soft brown sugar

2 teaspoons French mustard
1 small tin (8oz/225g) pineapple slices

1½lb (675g) loaf tin
Line a small baking tin or tray with foil.
Preheat oven to 350°F / Gas Mark 4 / 180°C.

Put the ground ham and pork into a large mixing bowl and mix in the onion, chopped finely. Soak the breadcrumbs and dissolve the mustard in the milk, then add to the meats. Season well with salt and pepper and bind together with the beaten egg. Press into the loaf tin and cover with foil. Bake in the centre of the oven for 30 minutes, then take out and reverse on to the lined tray.

While the loaf is cooking, put the butter in a bowl and soften with a wooden spoon. Add the brown sugar and cream together until light. Gradually mix in the mustard. Use to spread over the top and sides of the loaf (on the baking tray), then press the pineapple slices on top. Put back into the oven and cook for a further 30 minutes, basting frequently with the pan juices. Cool on a wire rack, then pack in a tin or plastic container. Serve sliced with green salad.

Serves 8

Beef and Pork

SWEET AND SOUR PORK

2–3 tablespoons vegetable oil
1 small green pepper
1 medium onion
1¼lb (675g) lean boneless pork
1 (8oz/225g) tin pineapple chunks
6oz (175ml) chicken stock

3oz (75g) soft brown sugar
3oz (75ml) vinegar
2 tablespoons soy sauce
2 teaspoons Worcestershire sauce
2 tablespoons cornflour
salt and pepper

Cooked rice for 4 people
Several aluminium-foil containers with lids or a wide-necked Thermos

Heat the oil in a large frying pan. Blanch the green pepper quickly in boiling water, then remove the pith and seeds and cut into thin strips. Peel the onion and slice thinly. Add both to the frying pan when the oil is hot and sauté until soft. Then cut the meat into medium chunks and add to the pan. Push the onion and pepper slices to one side and cook the meat quickly, browning on all sides. Lift vegetables and meat on to a square of absorbent kitchen paper and leave to drain off excess oil.

Pour 6oz (175ml) of the pineapple juice into a small saucepan with the chicken stock, soft brown sugar, vinegar, soy sauce and Worcestershire sauce. Blend the cornflour with a small amount of this mixture and then pour back into the pan. Mix well, then bring to the boil and cook for several minutes until slightly thickened. Stir in the meat, pineapple chunks, sliced onion and green pepper. Cover and simmer for 1 hour. Remove the lid and simmer for a further 30 minutes. Season to taste with salt and pepper.

Line the foil containers with the rice, pour the sweet and sour pork on top and cover with cardboard lids. Close tightly then put into a moderate oven until piping hot. Wrap in foil or several tea towels and transfer to an insulated bag. (If no insulated bag available, see introductory section on Keeping Food Hot.)

Serves 4

ORANGE-GLAZED HAM SLICES

6 gammon or bacon steaks (approx. ¼"/·50cm thick)

Glaze:

7 tablespoons orange juice grated rind of large orange
4 tablespoons brown sugar 2 teaspoons honey
2 teaspoons French mustard ½ teaspoon ground cloves
large pinch salt

Line a baking tray with foil.

Put all the glaze ingredients into a small saucepan and mix well. Bring slowly to the boil, then reduce the heat and simmer gently for 5 minutes.

Arrange the gammon steaks on the prepared tray. Coat with half the glaze and let stand (if there is time) for 30 minutes. Then put under a preheated grill (about 6"/15cm from it) for 5–10 minutes. Turn the steaks over, baste with the pan juices and coat with the remaining glaze. Grill for a further 5–10 minutes or until nicely browned. Transfer to a plastic container and spoon over any juices left in the pan. (Slice the steaks in half first for easier serving.) Cover with a lid and pack. Serve with brown rolls and sweetcorn and spring onion salad (or potato salad).

Serves 4–6

SPARERIBS WITH GINGER AND HONEY

1lb–2lb (450g–1kg) pork spareribs

Sauce:

1½ teaspoons soy sauce
2 tablespoons mango chutney
4 tablespoons lemon juice
6 tablespoons thick honey

1 teaspoon ground ginger
1 clove garlic
1 tablespoon olive or vegetable oil

2 tablespoons sherry

Line a large roasting tin with foil and put a rack on top.
Preheat oven to 350°F / Gas Mark 4 / 180°C.

Put all the sauce ingredients into a small saucepan (crush the garlic to a paste with a small amount of salt before adding). Bring to the boil, then reduce the heat and simmer gently for about 10 minutes. Check the seasoning and adjust if necessary. Then pour over the spareribs and leave to marinate for several hours or use straight away.

Put the ribs on the rack in the roasting tin (leave them as a whole piece: if you cut them into individual ribs at this point the meat will shrink). Brush well with the sauce and put into the oven. Cook for an hour, basting frequently. Then take out, cut between the bones to form 'fingers' and put into an aluminium container with a lid. Pack in an insulated bag. Or leave to cool on the rack and pack later in a lined tin or a plastic container.

Serves 4–6

SUKIYAKI

It's very important when preparing this dish to have all the ingredients ready beforehand. They must be cooked very quickly to retain their crispness.

1lb (450g) beef steak
½ large onion
10 large spring onions
4oz (100g) mushrooms
8oz (225g) Chinese cabbage
1 (16oz/450g) tin of bamboo shoots or bean sprouts

1oz (25ml) soy sauce
1 teaspoon sugar
1 teaspoon Worcestershire sauce
2oz (50ml) beef stock
2–3 tablespoons olive or vegetable oil
salt and pepper to taste

Cooked rice for 4 people
Aluminium-foil containers with lids

Slice the meat into thin lengthwise strips and put to one side. Cut the onion into thin slices. Wash the spring onions, top and tail them, then cut in half lengthwise. Wipe the mushrooms and slice thinly. Rinse the cabbage well and shred. Put the soy sauce, Worcestershire sauce, beef stock and sugar into a bowl and stir until well blended.

Heat the oil in a large frying pan and, when very hot, add the beef strips. Brown quickly on all sides, then push to one side of the pan. Add the sliced onions and sauté quickly until soft. Push to another part of the pan and cook the spring onions for several minutes. Push to one side and cook the Chinese cabbage and mushrooms in the same way. Try to keep the vegetables separated in the pan as much as possible. Put the bamboo shoots or bean sprouts in last with the beef stock mixture and cook over a high heat for 3–4 minutes.

Line a large aluminium-foil container (or several small ones) with cooked rice. Then cover with the sukiyaki, making sure that each container has a selection of all the vegetables. Pour the juices over and sprinkle with salt and pepper. Put the cardboard lids on tightly and place in a moderate oven until piping hot. Then pack in an insulated bag or wrap in foil and several layers of newspaper or tea towels.

Serves 4

CHINESE MEATBALLS (Quick)

1lb (450g) lean minced beef
1 egg
1 tablespoon dried onion flakes

1 teaspoon salt
½ teaspoon pepper
1 slice brown bread

Sauce:

4 tablespoons tomato ketchup
1½ tablespoons brown sugar
2 tablespoons water
1 tablespoon honey

1 tablespoon vinegar
1 tablespoon Worcestershire sauce
2 teaspoons French mustard

Preheat oven to 425°F / Gas Mark 7 / 220°C.

Put the minced beef, egg, onion flakes, salt and pepper into a large bowl. Tear the bread into small pieces and mix well with a fork. Shape the mixture into small balls and place in a roasting or baking tin. (If you're in a hurry, line this first with foil to save washing-up.)

In a small bowl, mix all the sauce ingredients together until smooth. Coat the meatballs well with it, then bake on the middle or top shelf of the oven for 15–20 minutes (be careful not to overcook: these should be slightly pink in the middle). Baste frequently with the sauce. Transfer to a plastic container and pack. Serve with salad as a main course or on toothpicks as an hors d'œuvre.

Makes 14–20 meatballs (depending on size)

Chicken

CHICKEN WITH BARBECUE SAUCE

8–10 chicken pieces (thighs, wings or legs)

Sauce:

1oz (25g) butter
1 medium onion
8 tablespoons tomato ketchup
3 tablespoons Worcestershire
   sauce

2 tablespoons brown sugar
1 tablespoon vinegar
1 teaspoon French mustard
1 teaspoon lemon juice
6oz (175ml) water

Line a small roasting tin or baking tray with foil.
Preheat oven to 375°F / Gas Mark 5 / 190°C.

Melt the butter in a medium saucepan and when foaming, add the onion, chopped finely. Sauté until just turning brown, then add all the remaining ingredients, except the lemon juice. Bring to the boil, then reduce the heat and simmer gently until the mixture is thick and syrupy (coating consistency). Take off the heat, stir in the lemon juice and check the seasoning.

Wipe the chicken dry with absorbent kitchen paper and place in lined tin. Use half the sauce to coat the chicken pieces, then cover the tin with foil and bake for 20 minutes. Take out, turn each piece over, baste with the pan juices and coat with the remaining sauce. Cook uncovered for a further 20 minutes, basting frequently. Then cook for 5 minutes on each side under a preheated grill (about 6"/15cm under it) until the chicken is nicely browned and crisp. Watch carefully as it can burn easily.

Put immediately into an aluminium-foil container and spoon over the pan juices. Cover with a cardboard lid and pack in an insulated bag. Or leave to cool on a wire rack (this drains excess grease) and pack later in foil or a plastic container.

Serves 4–6

LEMON CHICKEN

8 chicken pieces (thighs or legs)
1oz (25g) butter
1 large or 2 small lemons
$\frac{1}{4}$ pint (150ml) strong chicken stock

stock (or $\frac{1}{3}$ chicken stock cube dissolved in $\frac{1}{4}$ pint boiling water)
3 teaspoons sugar
salt and pepper

Melt the butter in a large frying pan and, when foaming, add the chicken pieces. Brown quickly on all sides to seal.

Pare the rind off the lemon with a potato peeler (taking care not to get any of the bitter white pith), then squeeze and strain all the juice. Mix with the chicken stock, sugar and a sprinkling of salt and pepper. Pour over the chicken and bring to the boil. Cover with a lid or foil and simmer gently for about 20 minutes, basting frequently. Remove the foil, check the seasoning and adjust if necessary. Then put about 6″ (15cm) under a hot grill* and cook the chicken for 5–10 minutes on each side or until the skin is crisp and golden. Baste with the pan juices then sprinkle with salt and pepper. Transfer to an aluminium-foil container, cover with a lid and pack in an insulated bag (or wrap in several tea towels or layers of damp newspaper). Or leave to cool on a wire rack, then pack in foil or a plastic container.

Serves 4–6

* If your frying pan has a wooden handle, transfer the chicken to a casserole dish before grilling.

POULET NORMAND
(Stuffed Chicken Breasts with Apples and Cider)

4 large chicken breasts
1$\frac{1}{2}$oz (40g) butter, at room temperature
1 small onion
1 dessert apple

salt and pepper
pinch of dried thyme
1 slice of white bread
3oz (75ml) medium or sweet cider
3oz (75ml) chicken stock

Dry the chicken breasts with absorbent kitchen paper, then carefully bone each one. Put, one at a time, between two sheets of lightly oiled greaseproof paper and pound flat with a meat mallet or rolling pin.

Melt 1oz (25g) of the butter in a small frying pan and add the onion, chopped finely. Cook until soft and transparent, then transfer the onion and the pan juices to a mixing bowl. Peel, core and chop the apple into small dice and add to the onion with salt, pepper and a pinch of dried thyme. Crumble a slice of white bread into the bowl and mix in well. (If the mixture seems dry, add a small amount of melted butter to bind it together.)

Put a thin strip of filling down the centre of each chicken escalope and roll up tightly from the long side. Put seam side down and tie widthwise in three places with short pieces of string. Put into a small roasting tin (rounded side up) and rub the skins with the remaining butter. Mix the cider and chicken stock together and pour over. Bake at 375°F/Gas Mark 5/190°C for an hour, basting from time to time. Cool on a wire rack and, when completely cold, remove the string. Pack in a plastic container or wrap in foil or cling film. Serve whole or sliced widthwise. Delicious with ice-cold cider and french bean and bacon salad.

Serves 4

CORONATION CHICKEN

One version of the dish created by the Cordon Bleu School to honour the coronation of Elizabeth II.

6oz (175g) long-grain rice, cooked
8 large cooked chicken breasts
½oz (15g) butter
1 medium onion
2 teaspoons curry powder
1 tablespoon tomato purée

5oz (150ml) chicken stock
3 tablespoons mango chutney
2 tablespoons apricot jam
2 teaspoons lemon juice
8–10 tablespoons mayonnaise
4 tablespoons single cream
salt and pepper
paprika

130

Melt the butter in a frying pan and add the onion, chopped finely. Cook until soft and about to turn colour. Then stir in the curry powder and cook for a minute or two. Pour in the chicken stock and mix well. Blend in the tomato purée, chutney and apricot jam. Simmer over moderate heat until thick, then add the lemon juice and a small amount of salt and pepper. Strain and put into the refrigerator or freezer to cool slightly.

Remove the skin and bones, then chop the chicken into small bite-size pieces. Put the cooled sauce in a large bowl and gradually whisk in the mayonnaise and cream. Fold in the chicken pieces and blend well. Line a plastic container or plate with the cooked rice and arrange the chicken on top. Sprinkle with paprika and cover with a lid or foil. (Try, if you can, to make this the day before as it gives the flavours a chance to develop fully.)

Serves 4

CHICKEN COTE D'OR (Quick)

8 chicken pieces (thighs or legs)   3½ tablespoons thick honey
2oz (50g) butter   4 tablespoons sherry
4 tablespoons Dijon mustard   Salt and pepper to taste

Preheat oven to 375°F / Gas Mark 5 / 190°C.

Melt the butter in a small saucepan and stir in the mustard, honey and sherry. Heat slowly until boiling, then reduce the heat and simmer for several minutes until slightly thickened (stirring occasionally). Season lightly with salt and pepper.

Wipe the chicken pieces dry and put close together in a small roasting tin. Coat with two-thirds of the sauce and bake for 20 minutes, basting from time to time. Turn the chicken over and coat with half the remaining sauce. Cook for a further 15 minutes, basting frequently. Then coat with the rest of the sauce and put under the grill (about 6"/15cm from it) and grill each side until well browned and crispy. Take out, put into an aluminium-foil container and spoon over the pan juices. Cover with a lid and pack in an insulated bag. Or leave to cool on a rack and pack later in foil or a plastic container. Sprinkle the chicken with salt and pepper before packing or hand round separately when serving.

Serves 4

Fish

STUFFED TROUT OR BASS

4 small trout

1oz (25g) soft butter

Stuffing:

1oz (25g) butter
2 shallots or baby onions
1 large stalk celery
half a bunch of watercress (use
  the rest as garnish)

1 tablespoon chopped parsley
  (fresh or dried)
large pinch of dried basil
salt and pepper
2 slices of bread

1 small egg

Preheat the oven to 350°F / Gas Mark 4 / 180°C.

Melt an ounce (25g) of butter in a frying pan and sauté the shallots (chopped finely) until soft and transparent. Then transfer with the pan juices to a small bowl. Add the celery, washed and chopped into small dice, and the watercress, shredded finely. Mix in the parsley, basil, salt and pepper. Slice the crusts off the bread, tear into small pieces and mix in. Beat the egg lightly and use to bind the mixture together. Check the seasoning and adjust if necessary.

Wash and clean the trout, then dry well. Put on a double

square of absorbent kitchen paper, stuff generously with the watercress filling and secure with string or toothpicks cut in half. Rub with the soft butter, sprinkle with salt and pepper and wrap loosely in foil. Put on a baking tray and bake in the centre of the oven for 35–40 minutes. Take out and pack at once in an insulated bag or leave to cool in the foil.

Serves 4

BAKED MACKEREL WITH MUSTARD SAUCE

4 small mackerel
1oz (25g) butter

a good squeeze of lemon juice
salt and freshly ground pepper

Sauce:
2 large egg yolks
1½ teaspoons soft brown sugar
1 tablespoon French mustard
2–3 tablespoons white wine
 vinegar

2–3 tablespoons of olive or
 vegetable oil
1–2 tablespoons of boiling
 water

Preheat the oven to 350°F / Gas Mark 4 / 180°C.

Wash and clean the mackerel thoroughly. Dry with kitchen paper, then rub with butter and sprinkle with salt and freshly ground pepper. Put on a double square of foil, give a good squeeze of lemon juice and wrap up loosely (but making sure that it is airtight). Put on a baking tray and bake in the centre of the oven for about 40 minutes. Pack at once in an insulated bag or leave to cool in the foil.

To make the sauce, put the egg yolks into a small saucepan. Add the sugar and whisk until well blended. Then whisk in the mustard and 1 tablespoon of vinegar. Add the oil, drop by drop, with the saucepan over gentle heat, whisking all the time. Then add the remaining vinegar and continue whisking until thick.

133

Take off the heat and whisk in the boiling water (adding more if too thick). Transfer to a small dish, cover with a piece of dampened greaseproof paper and leave to cool. Remove the paper, cover with cling film and pack.

Serves 4

TROUT OR MULLET 'EN PAPILLOTE' (Quick)

4 small trout or mullet

Maître d'Hôtel Butter:

1oz (25g) butter
1 teaspoon finely chopped
parsley

1 teaspoon lemon juice
salt and pepper

Preheat the oven to 350°F / Gas Mark 4 / 180°C.

Soften the butter with a wooden spoon, then cream until light. Add the parsley, salt and pepper, then gradually whisk in the lemon juice. Mould into a sausage shape about $1\frac{1}{2}''$ (3·5cm) in diameter and wrap in greaseproof paper. Chill until firm (this takes 30 minutes to an hour).

Wash and clean the trout thoroughly and dry with kitchen paper. Then put on to a piece of heavy-duty foil or a double layer of the ordinary kind. Cut several slices of the maître d'hôtel butter and put inside the cavity of each fish, then place one or two more on the top. Sprinkle well with salt and pepper then wrap completely in the foil. Bake in the centre of the oven for 30–40 minutes, depending on size. Take out and pack immediately in an insulated bag or leave to cool in the foil.

Serves 4

GRILLED MULLET (Quick)

4 small red mullet
1 fennel bulb

1oz–2oz (25g–50g) butter,
melted
juice of 1 lemon

Wash and clean the mullet thoroughly, then dry with absorbent kitchen paper. Remove the outer skin of the fennel and slice into thin pieces. Make several diagonal incisions down each side of the mullet and insert a piece of fennel into each. Place on a baking tray and pour lemon juice over each one. Then brush generously with melted butter. Put under a preheated grill and cook for 5–10 minutes each side, brushing again with butter as you turn. Then sprinkle with salt and pepper. Wrap at once in a double layer of foil and pack (or leave to cool in the foil).

Serves 4

Recipes for the following are given in other parts of the book: Veal Cake (p. 211), Potted Chicken (p. 211), Potted Beef (p. 219), Shrimp Creole (p. 250).

We came upon a cave or recess in the side of a huge mass of rock, forming a spacious apartment, and were very agreeably surprised at seeing a table spread with tea, coffee, cold ham, fowls and other articles of food, all of the best kind.

from *William Hickey's Diaries (1749–1808)*

8

SALADS

Let it be laid down as a golden rule, that the concoction
of a salad should never, or hardly ever, be entrusted
to the tender mercies of the British serving-maid. For the
salad-maker, like the poet, is born, not made; and the
divine afflatus – I don't mean garlic – is as essential in the
one as in the other.

Edward Spencer in *Cakes and Ale* (1897)

Of all picnic foods, salad seems to suffer the most. If the perils
of transportation don't leave it limp and soggy, then an overdose
of salad dressing frequently does. But with careful preparation
and packing this can be avoided and an infinite variety of salads
can arrive at the picnic with all their freshness and flavour intact.

Salad Tips

****** Always dry greens after washing in several layers of
absorbent kitchen paper to remove excess moisture. Then wrap
in a clean tea towel or double layer of kitchen paper and put
into a large polythene bag. Refrigerate until needed, then pack.

****** Pack the dressing in a separate container (small mustard,
honey or jam jars are ideal for this) and add to the salad just
before serving. (Unless, of course, the recipe specifically says to
add it before. Some mixed salads improve in flavour if allowed
to marinate in the dressing for several hours or overnight.)

****** To avoid losing or forgetting the salad dressing altogether, wrap the jar in a piece of absorbent kitchen paper, place in the centre of the salad bowl and surround with salad ingredients. The weight of the greens will keep it from toppling over and if the lid is on tightly it should come to no harm. Cover the bowl with cling film and pack. Remove the covering just before serving, pour the dressing over the salad and toss.

****** Salads packed in a plastic container should be placed near the bottom of the picnic basket or bag so that they can rest on the ice-packs. Those in a salad bowl should be packed near the top so the greens aren't crushed.

****** Don't try to fit too much salad into a container. Pack it as loosely as possible so that it has a chance to breathe. If it is squashed, it will become limp and soggy very quickly.

****** If there is an ingredient in the salad which is likely to lose its crispness (e.g. croûtons), then carry it separately in a polythene bag and add at the last minute.

****** Any salad containing avocado, banana or apple should contain a small amount of lemon juice to prevent discolouration.

Dressings

MAYONNAISE

For the best results, all the ingredients should be at room temperature and a whisk should be used for mixing.

1 large egg yolk
large pinch of dry mustard
pinch of caster sugar
salt and pepper

$\frac{1}{4}$ pint (150ml) olive or vegetable oil
1 tablespoon lemon juice or wine vinegar

Put the egg yolk, seasonings and sugar into a small bowl and whisk until thick. Add the oil drop by drop until half has been added (it should then be quite thick). Then add 1 teaspoon of the vinegar or lemon juice and blend in. Pour in the remaining oil in a thin, steady stream, whisking all the time. When it has all been added, whisk in the remaining vinegar (or lemon juice) and check the seasoning. If it seems too thick, whisk in 1 table-spoon of boiling water. Turn into a jar or bowl, cover tightly and refrigerate.

Makes ¼ pint (150ml)

BLENDER MAYONNAISE

2 egg yolks
large pinch of mustard
salt and pepper
2 tablespoons lemon juice or
   wine vinegar

½ pint (275ml) olive or
   vegetable oil
1–2 tablespoons boiling water

Put the egg yolks, seasonings and vinegar (or lemon juice) into the blender. Whizz on low speed until well blended. Then take off the centre cap of the lid and, with the blender on low speed, pour in the oil drop by drop. When the mayonnaise thickens, pour in the oil in a steady stream until it has all been incor-porated (stopping occasionally to scrape down the sides of the blender). Then pour in the boiling water and blend for several seconds. Check the seasoning and adjust if necessary. Put into a screw-top jar or bowl (cover tightly) and refrigerate until needed.

Makes ½ pint (275ml)

OLD-FASHIONED SALAD DRESSING

1 teaspoon dry mustard
1½ tablespoons sugar
½ teaspoon salt
2 level tablespoons flour
¼ teaspoon paprika

4oz (100ml) water
1 egg
1½oz (40ml) vinegar
1oz (25g) butter

Mix the mustard, sugar, salt, flour and paprika together in a small bowl, then gradually blend in the water. Put the egg and vinegar into a basin over hot water. Whisk until smooth, then mix in the flour mixture. Cook over simmering water until thick, stirring frequently. Take off the heat, blend in the butter thoroughly, then pour into a screw-top jar. Cover with a dampened piece of greaseproof paper and refrigerate until needed.

Makes ¼ pint (150ml)

BACON DRESSING

2–3 rashers of streaky bacon
1 egg
1½ teaspoons sugar
2½ tablespoons vinegar

3 tablespoons oil
salt and black pepper
2 tablespoons boiling water

Cook the bacon rashers until crisp, drain on kitchen paper, then crumble into small pieces. Cool the bacon fat slightly, then put in a basin fitted in a saucepan filled with a small quantity of hot water. Put over low heat, then stir in the egg, lightly beaten, with the sugar. Whisk until smooth, then continue whisking while adding half the oil, drop by drop. Add half the vinegar, blend well and take off the heat. Add the remaining oil in a steady stream, then the rest of the vinegar. Return to the heat and whisk until thick. Whisk in the boiling water (adding more if necessary to get the right consistency) and blend until smooth. Then season to taste with salt and pepper. Mix in the crumbled bacon, then pour into a small jar or plastic container and cover with a dampened piece of greaseproof paper. Refrigerate for several hours before using. (Dilute if necessary with a tablespoon of boiling water.)

Makes a scant ¼ pint (150ml)

CLASSIC VINAIGRETTE

2 tablespoons wine vinegar
6 tablespoons olive or
  vegetable oil
salt and pepper

1 tablespoon chopped fresh
  herbs (parsley, thyme,
  chives)

Put all the ingredients into a screw-top jar, close tightly and shake vigorously until well blended. Check the seasoning and adjust if necessary.

Makes a scant ¼ pint (150ml)

FRENCH DRESSING

1½ teaspoons brown sugar
1 teaspoon French mustard
1 teaspoon chopped dried
  herbs

2 tablespoons wine vinegar
6 tablespoons olive or
  vegetable oil
salt and pepper

Put all the ingredients into a screw-top jar, close tightly and shake vigorously until blended. Check the seasoning and adjust if necessary.

Makes a scant ¼ pint (150ml)

BLENDER FRENCH DRESSING

½ teaspoon paprika
2 teaspoons French mustard
1 small onion
2 tablespoons lemon juice
3 tablespoons wine vinegar

1 tablespoon dried mixed
  herbs
1 tablespoon sugar
½ pint (275ml) olive or
  vegetable oil

salt and pepper

Put all the ingredients into the blender and mix on medium speed until smooth and well blended. Check the seasoning and adjust if necessary.

Makes $\frac{1}{2}$ pint (275ml)

ARCADIAN DRESSING

2 tablespoons wine vinegar	6 tablespoons tomato ketchup
2 tablespoons lemon juice	8 tablespoons olive or
large pinch sugar	vegetable oil
	salt and pepper

Put all the ingredients into a screw-top jar, close tightly, and shake vigorously until blended. Check the seasoning. (Do not make this dressing in a blender as it will alter the colour and consistency).

Makes $\frac{1}{4}$ pint (150ml)

A selection of Mrs Beeton's salad dressings can be found in *Mr Cheesacre's Picnic* (pp. 223–4).

Vegetable Salads

GREEN SALAD

1–2 fresh lettuces (any type)	chopped fresh herbs

Vinaigrette or French dressing

Wash the lettuces, drain well and dry in kitchen paper. Tear into pieces, then put into a salad bowl with the chopped herbs. Cover with cling film and pack. Toss with French or vinaigrette dressing just before serving.

MIXED GREEN SALAD

1 large lettuce
1 green pepper
½ large cucumber
8 large spring onions

4oz (100g) cooked green beans
  or peas
2 large stalks celery

French or Vinaigrette dressing

Wash and drain the lettuce well. Shake to remove excess moisture or dry in absorbent kitchen paper. Wash the celery and cucumber and cut into small chunks. Remove the outer skin of the spring onions and chop finely. Chop the beans into more manageable lengths or leave as is. Slice the top off the pepper, remove the pith and seeds and cut into thin strips. Put all the ingredients into a salad bowl, cover with cling film and pack. Toss with French or vinaigrette dressing just before serving.

MIXED SALAD

1 large lettuce
4 ripe tomatoes
2 large stalks celery
4 radishes

small chicory
small green pepper
6 spring onions
½ cucumber

French or Vinaigrette dressing

Wash and drain the lettuce, then shake to remove excess moisture or dry with absorbent kitchen paper. Tear into pieces and put in a salad bowl. Wash and dry the tomatoes, cut into quarters and add. Top and tail the radishes, then slice thinly. Wash and dry the cucumber, then cut into thin slices or small chunks. Shred the chicory and chop the washed celery into small dice. Slice the top off the green pepper, remove the pith and seeds and chop into thin strips. Mix all of these in with the lettuce, then cover the bowl with cling film and pack. Add the French or vinaigrette dressing just before serving and toss well.

SPINACH SALAD WITH MANDARINS

1 large head of Webb lettuce
1lb (450g) fresh spinach

1 (11oz/312g) tin mandarin oranges

Arcadian or French dressing

Wash the spinach and lettuce thoroughly, drain and dry well in absorbent kitchen paper. Tear into bite-size pieces, then wrap in a double layer of kitchen paper or a clean tea towel and put into a large polythene bag. Drain the mandarin oranges and put into a small plastic container. Put this and the bag of lettuce and spinach into the salad bowl and pack.

Make up the Arcadian or French dressing (see pp. 140–1 for recipes) in a screw-top jar. Pack in the salad bowl with the other ingredients. Just before serving, empty the bag of greens into the bowl, add the mandarins and the dressing and toss well.

Serves 8–10

SWEETCORN AND SPRING ONION SALAD

2 (11½oz/326g) tins of sweet-corn

1 large bunch of spring onions

Dressing:

1 teaspoon French mustard
1 teaspoon sugar
2 tablespoons wine vinegar

6 tablespoons olive or vegetable oil
salt and freshly ground pepper

Drain the sweetcorn, then tip into a mixing bowl. Wash the spring onions and remove the outer layer, then chop finely. Add to the sweetcorn and mix well.

Put all the dressing ingredients into a screw-top jar and mix thoroughly. Check the seasoning and adjust if necessary. Pour over the salad and toss well. Sprinkle the salad generously with salt and black pepper. Cover with cling film and refrigerate until needed.

Serves 6

CARROT AND RAISIN SALAD

This salad is one which improves if made the day before. The sultanas plump up, the carrots soften slightly, and the flavours become more distinct.

2lb (1kg) fresh carrots   6oz (175g) sultanas

Dressing:
½ teaspoon French mustard   2 teaspoons dried parsley
1½ teaspoons sugar   salt and black pepper
2 tablespoons wine vinegar
6 tablespoons olive or
  vegetable oil

Peel the carrots and cut into thin julienne strips (about 1½"/ 3·5cm long). Put into a large bowl and mix in the sultanas.

Put all the dressing ingredients into a screw-top jar and mix thoroughly. Check the seasoning, then pour over the salad and toss well. Cover the bowl with cling film and refrigerate for several hours or overnight. Toss again before packing and then just before serving.

Serves 6–8

TOMATO SALAD

1lb (450g) small ripe firm   1 small onion
  tomatoes   chopped fresh herbs

Dressing:

1 teaspoon French mustard
1 teaspoon white sugar
2 tablespoons white wine
  vinegar

6 tablespoons olive or
  vegetable oil
salt and pepper

Wash the tomatoes and dry well with kitchen paper. Then slice across, but not too thinly as this will make them more likely to split. Put into a plastic container with freshly chopped herbs and the onion, sliced very thinly. Sprinkle well with salt and freshly ground black pepper. Put all the dressing ingredients into a small jar and shake vigorously until well blended. Then pour over the salad and toss gently, using two spoons. Cover with a lid and refrigerate until needed. Toss again just before serving.

Serves 4

POTATO SALAD

1½lb (675g) new potatoes

spring onions or chives

Dressing:

1 teaspoon Dijon mustard
1 teaspoon sugar
2 tablespoons white wine
  vinegar
6 tablespoons olive or
  vegetable oil

2 tablespoons mayonnaise
salt and lots of black pepper
squeeze of lemon juice

Cook the new potatoes in salted water until just tender, being careful not to overcook. Pour into a colander and leave for several minutes to drain. Then slice thinly (while still warm) and put into a bowl with a handful of chopped spring onions or chives. Put all the dressing ingredients into a small screw-top jar and shake vigorously until well blended. Pour over the potatoes and toss carefully, using two spoons. Transfer to a

smaller bowl or plastic container, cover with a lid or cling film
and pack.

Serves 4

FRENCH BEAN AND BACON SALAD

1lb (450g) whole french beans (fresh or frozen)

4 rashers of streaky bacon

French dressing:
½ small onion, chopped finely
1 teaspoon French mustard
1 teaspoon sugar
2 tablespoons vinegar

6 tablespoons olive or vegetable oil
pinch of parsley or dried mixed herbs
salt and black pepper

Put a small amount of water into a saucepan, salt generously
and bring to a rapid boil. Add the beans and cook for 4–5
minutes or until just tender (be careful not to overcook). Pour
straight into a colander and leave to drain completely. Then put
into a small salad or mixing bowl and season well with salt and
freshly ground black pepper.

Cook the bacon rashers until crisp and drain on kitchen paper.
Crumble or cut into small pieces and sprinkle over the beans.
Put all the dressing ingredients into a blender or screw-top jar
and mix thoroughly. Pour over the beans and toss well. Cover
the bowl with cling film and chill until needed.

Serves 4

CHOUFLEUR POLONAIS

1 large cauliflower
3–5 tablespoons olive or vegetable oil
1–2 tablespoons dried breadcrumbs

1 tablespoon dried parsley
salt and black pepper

146

Wash the cauliflower and cut into small florets. Cook in boiling salted water until almost tender. Then pour into a colander and drain well.

Heat the oil in a large frying pan until almost sizzling. Add the cauliflower and cook quickly until nicely browned on all sides. Turn carefully using two spoons and shake the pan frequently to keep the cauliflower from sticking (if it gets too dry, add more oil). Lift out of the pan with a fish slice and put into a small bowl or plastic container. Sprinkle with the breadcrumbs and parsley and toss lightly. Season with salt and freshly ground black pepper.

Serves 4

Special Salads

FRENCH APPLE, DATE AND ASPARAGUS SALAD

4 French golden delicious apples
1 (12oz/340g) tin asparagus

4oz (100g) dates
4oz (100g) cheddar cheese

French dressing:
1 teaspoon French mustard
1 teaspoon sugar
1 tablespoon lemon juice
1 tablespoon vinegar

6 tablespoons of olive or vegetable oil
salt and freshly ground black pepper

Remove the stones from the dates and cut into thin strips lengthwise. Cut the cheddar into small dice. Wash and dry the apples, then core and chop into small chunks. Put all of these into a salad bowl, with the asparagus spears on top.

Put the dressing ingredients into a screw-top jar. Shake vigorously until well blended, then pour over the salad. Mix carefully, using two spoons. Cover the bowl with cling film and pack. Toss lightly again before serving.

Serves 6–8

EGG, CROUTON AND CRESS SALAD

This is a delicious combination but one that is more perishable than most and should be made just before leaving for the picnic.

4 thick slices of wholemeal bread	1 bunch watercress
5 large eggs	1 bunch mustard and cress
2oz (50g) butter	salt and freshly ground black pepper

1 tablespoon vegetable or olive oil

Remove the crusts and cut the bread into small squares. Put on a baking tray and into a moderate oven (350°F / Gas Mark 4 / 180°C) to dry out and brown slightly.

Heat the butter and oil in a large frying pan and add the lightly browned croûtons, tossing well in the mixture. Cook over medium heat until well browned, then transfer to the baking tray and leave in the oven (at a low temperature) until needed.

Wash the mustard and cress and cut it (using kitchen scissors) into a medium serving or salad bowl. Rinse and drain the watercress well. Then shred and add to the bowl. Put the eggs in a saucepan of water, bring to the boil and boil for $3\frac{1}{2}$ minutes exactly. (The whites should be firm but the yolks still slightly soft.) Take out and put into a bowl of cold water. Unpeel them as quickly as possible, chop finely and add to the salad bowl. Take the croûtons out of the oven and toss well with the other ingredients. Add salt and black pepper to taste. Cover with cling film and pack.

Serves 4

CABBAGE AND RED APPLE COLESLAW

1 small green cabbage
4 red dessert apples

1 small onion

Dressing:

1 teaspoon sugar
1 tablespoon lemon juice
2 tablespoons olive or
  vegetable oil

6 tablespoons mayonnaise
1 tablespoon chopped fresh or
  dried parsley
salt and pepper

Shred the cabbage, rinse well under ice-cold water and leave to drain. Wash and dry the apples with kitchen paper, then core and cut into thin slices (leave the skin on). Chop the onion finely and put into a large salad bowl with the apples and cabbage.

Mix all the dressing ingredients together in a screw-top jar, then pour over the salad and mix well. Check the seasoning and adjust if necessary. Cover the bowl with cling film and refrigerate until needed.

Serves 8–10

Pasta and Rice Salads

RICE SALAD WITH ONION AND BACON

8oz (225g) long-grained rice
1oz (25g) butter
1 medium onion
4 rashers of streaky bacon
1¼ pints (700ml) chicken stock
salt and pepper

2–3 tablespoons of olive or
  vegetable oil
freshly chopped parsley

Preheat the oven to 350°F / Gas Mark 4 / 180°C.

Chop the onion and bacon finely, then sauté in the butter until the onion is soft and just turning colour. Add the rice and cook for several minutes, stirring constantly. Pour in the chicken stock, mix well and bring to the boil. Transfer the mixture to a casserole dish, add salt and pepper and stir again. Cover tightly and cook in the centre of the oven for 20–30 minutes or until all the liquid has been absorbed, leaving the rice light and fluffy. Take out, sprinkle with chopped parsley, and pack at once in a warmed wide-necked Thermos. Or leave to cool, then stir in several tablespoons of olive or vegetable oil and spoon into a plastic container. Sprinkle with chopped parsley, cover with a lid and pack.

Serves 4–6

SAFFRON SALAD WITH NUTS AND RAISINS

1 teaspoon French mustard	chopped parsley (fresh or dried)
1 teaspoon sugar	4oz (100g) salted peanuts
1 tablespoon white wine vinegar	4oz (100g) sultanas or raisins
4 tablespoons vegetable or olive oil	8oz (225g) uncooked rice
salt and pepper	large pinch saffron (or turmeric)

Mix the mustard, sugar, vinegar, oil, salt, pepper and chopped parsley together in a small jar. Pour into a bowl and add the peanuts and raisins. Stir until they are well coated in the mixture, then put to one side.

Cook the rice with a large pinch of saffron or turmeric according to the instructions on the packet. Pour into a sieve, rinse well with hot water and leave to drain (stirring occasionally with a fork to prevent sticking). When fluffy and dry, mix in with the nuts and raisins and toss well. Check the seasoning and adjust if necessary. If the salad seems a bit dry, add another tablespoon of oil. Transfer to a plastic container, cover with a lid and pack.

Serves 4–6

PASTA SALAD WITH AUBERGINES

6oz (175g) pasta shells
2 large aubergines

1 large onion

Sauce:
1oz (25g) butter
2 level tablespoons flour
½ pint (275ml) milk
3oz (75g) cheddar cheese

2–4 tablespoons olive or
vegetable oil

chopped parsley (fresh or
dried)
1–2 tablespoons olive or
vegetable oil
salt and pepper

Put about 3 pints (1·5 litres) of water into a large saucepan, salt generously, and bring to a rolling boil. Add the pasta shells and cook until they are 'al dente' (just soft enough to be cut with a fingernail). Pour into a colander or sieve, and rinse through with hot water. Separate any shells that have become stuck together.

Put the oil into a large frying pan and, when hot, add the onion, chopped finely, and the aubergine which has been cut into small dice. Cook over moderate heat, stirring frequently until both are soft and just turning colour (this takes 15–20 minutes).

While the aubergine is cooking, prepare the sauce. Melt the butter in a small saucepan, stir in the flour and cook for 1 minute. Take off the heat, stir in the milk and cook over moderate heat until it comes to the boil. Reduce the heat and add salt, pepper and the cheese. Mix until the cheese is thoroughly blended, then stir in the onion and aubergine. Pour this mixture over the pasta shells and mix in well. *To serve hot:* Spoon into a warmed wide-necked Thermos, sprinkle with chopped parsley, close tightly and pack. *To serve cold:* Leave to cool, then carefully mix in 1–2 tablespoons of olive or vegetable oil. Spoon the salad into a plastic container and sprinkle with chopped parsley. Cover with a lid and pack.

Serves 4–6

PASTA SALAD WITH TOMATOES, CELERY AND CUCUMBER

6oz (175g) uncooked pasta shells
½ small cucumber
1 large stalk celery

½ large green pepper
6 firm ripe tomatoes
chopped parsley or dried herbs

Dressing:

1 teaspoon chopped herbs
1 teaspoon French mustard
1½ teaspoons sugar
1 tablespoon finely chopped onion
2 tablespoons tomato ketchup

2 tablespoons mayonnaise
1 tablespoon white wine vinegar
2 tablespoons olive or vegetable oil
salt and lots of black pepper

Wash the cucumber and wipe dry with kitchen paper. Then chop into small chunks, put on a plate and sprinkle generously with salt. Leave for at least 30 minutes, then pour off the liquid and dry with kitchen paper.

Cook the pasta shells in 3 pints (1·5 litres) of salted, rapidly boiling water until they are 'al dente' (just soft enough to be cut with a fingernail). Pour into a colander or sieve, rinse well with hot water and leave to drain completely. (Separate any shells that might have become stuck together.)

Wash the celery and slice into short, thin julienne strips. Blanch the green pepper quickly in boiling water, refresh under cold water, then slice off the top and remove the pith and seeds. Cut into short, thin strips. Wash the tomatoes and wipe dry. Slice carefully into quarters or eighths.

Mix the pasta (it should be quite dry) and the vegetables lightly together in a medium bowl. Put all the dressing ingredients into a screw-top jar and shake vigorously until smooth. Check the seasoning, then pour over the salad. Toss carefully, using two spoons, and season well with salt and freshly ground black pepper. Sprinkle with chopped parsley or chopped herbs. Cover with cling film and pack. (This salad must be made the day of the picnic.) Toss again just before serving.

Serves 4–6

Main Course Salads

CHICKEN SALAD WITH GRAPES AND WALNUTS

4 large cooked chicken breasts
2 large stalks celery
2oz (50g) chopped walnuts

8oz (225g) black or green grapes (or a mixture of both)

Dressing:
½ teaspoon French mustard
½ teaspoon sugar
1 teaspoon finely chopped onion

1 tablespoon tarragon vinegar
3 tablespoons olive oil
4 tablespoons mayonnaise
salt and pepper

Remove the skin and bone from the chicken breasts, then cut into bite-size chunks. Wash the celery and dry in kitchen paper. Cut into medium dice and put into a mixing bowl with the chicken and chopped walnuts. Wash and dry the grapes well, then halve and remove the pips. Add to the bowl with the other ingredients.

Mix the dressing ingredients together in a small jar, then pour over the salad and toss well. Season to taste with salt and pepper. Transfer to a salad bowl or plastic container, cover with a lid or cling film and refrigerate until needed.

Serves 4

CHEF'S SALAD

1 large Cos or Webb lettuce	3oz (75g) cheddar cheese
1 large cooked chicken breast	2 hard-boiled eggs
2 slices of cooked ham	3 spring onions
4 large tomatoes	4 rashers of streaky bacon

Bacon or Arcadian dressing

Wash and dry the lettuce. Cut the ham into julienne strips, the tomatoes into quarters, and the cheese into small cubes. Cook the bacon until crisp, drain well on kitchen paper, then crumble into small pieces. Remove the skin and bone of the chicken and cut the flesh into bite-size pieces. Chop the spring onions and egg finely.

Tear the lettuce into smaller pieces and put in a salad bowl. Arrange the chicken, cheese, ham and tomato sections on top, then sprinkle with the chopped onions, egg and crumbled bacon. Season lightly with salt and black pepper. Cover the bowl with cling film and pack. Toss in bacon or Arcadian dressing just before serving.

Serves 6–8

SALADE NICOISE

2 heads of Cos lettuce or 1 large Webb lettuce	1 small tin (2oz/50g) anchovy fillets
4oz (100g) green beans	4 ripe tomatoes
3 large hard-boiled eggs	8–10 black olives
1 (7oz/200g) tin of tuna	

French dressing:

1 teaspoon French mustard	salt and black pepper
1 teaspoon sugar	chopped herbs (dried or fresh)
2 tablespoons wine vinegar	
6 tablespoons olive or vegetable oil	

Wash and drain the lettuce well. Dry in absorbent kitchen paper, then tear into small pieces and put in a large salad bowl. Put the anchovies on a saucer, cover with milk and put to one side. Cook the green beans in a small amount of generously salted boiling water for 4–5 minutes. Drain well, then add to the lettuce. Pour the oil off the tuna and drain on kitchen paper. Flake into bite-size pieces and arrange in a circle round the edge of the bowl. Boil the eggs until hard, put into cold water and remove the shells. Cut into quarters and arrange pinwheel fashion on top of the lettuce. Put a few olives in the centre and the rest round the edges. Wash and dry the tomatoes, then cut into quarters and put in between the egg slices. Drain the anchovies, dry on kitchen paper and add to the salad. Cover the bowl with cling film. Mix all the dressing ingredients together in a screw-top jar and add to the salad just before serving.

Serves 4–6 (as a main course), 6–8 (as an hors d'œuvre)

PRAWN SALAD

3oz (75g) rice
4oz–6oz (100g–175g) prawns
8oz (225g) cooked peas
3 stalks celery

1 small green pepper
4 spring onions
chopped parsley (fresh or dried)

Dressing:

1 teaspoon French mustard
1 teaspoon sugar
2 tablespoons white wine vinegar

6 tablespoons olive or vegetable oil
salt and pepper
chopped herbs (fresh or dried)

Cook the rice according to the instructions on the packet. Pour in a sieve and leave until dry and fluffy (stir with a fork from time to time to prevent sticking). Put all the dressing ingredients into a small screw-top jar and shake vigorously until well blended. Pour into a medium bowl.

Wash the vegetables thoroughly. Remove the pith and seeds from the green pepper and cut into short, thin strips. Chop the spring onions finely and cut the celery into small dice. Put in the bowl with the dressing. Add the prawns (if using frozen ones, make sure they are completely thawed and well drained of water first) and cooked peas. Mix well and leave to marinate in the dressing for 20–30 minutes. Then fold in the rice and season to taste with salt and pepper. Transfer to a bowl or plastic container and sprinkle with chopped parsley. Cover with a lid or cling film and pack.

Serves 4–6

Fruit Salads

PEAR AND BLACK GRAPE SALAD

1lb (450g) black grapes
4 large or 5 small firm ripe
 pears
6 small 'rounds' of 'Petit
 Suisse' cheese
5–6 tablespoons milk
1 teaspoon lemon juice

2–3 tablespoons sugar
 (or to taste)
1 tablespoon vegetable or
 olive oil
 or 1 tablespoon vinaigrette
 dressing
chopped mint (optional)

Wash the grapes and dry well in absorbent kitchen paper. Halve, remove the pips and put into a mixing bowl. Wash and dry the pears, then remove the cores and slice lengthwise. Add to the grapes.

Put the 'Petit Suisse' cheese into a bowl and add just enough milk to give a coating consistency. Mix in the lemon juice, sugar (to your own taste) and the olive oil or vinaigrette dressing. Pour over the fruit and toss lightly. Transfer to a plastic container, cover with the lid and refrigerate until needed. (To give a touch of colour, sprinkle with chopped mint just before serving.)

Serves 4

ORANGE AND CELERY SALAD

4 large oranges
8 large stalks celery
salt and pepper

Dressing:

½ teaspoon French mustard
1 teaspoon sugar
1½ tablespoons white wine
  vinegar

2 tablespoons olive or
  vegetable oil
5 tablespoons mayonnaise
salt and pepper

Peel the oranges and slice thinly lengthwise. Remove the seeds and any white pith, then put into a medium bowl.

Wash the celery and dry well with absorbent kitchen paper. Slice into thin julienne strips, about 1″ (2·5cm) long, and add to the oranges.

Put all the dressing ingredients, except the salt and pepper, into a screw-top jar and shake vigorously until well blended. Pour over the salad and toss well. Cover with cling film and refrigerate until needed. (This salad should be made the day of the picnic.) Season to taste with salt and pepper just before serving.

Serves 4–6

WALDORF SALAD

4 shiny red apples
  (approx. 1lb/450g in weight)
2 large stalks celery
2oz (50g) chopped walnuts
2oz (50g) raisins or sultanas

4 tablespoons of Old-fashioned
  Dressing
and 4 tablespoons of cream
or 10 tablespoons of mayonnaise

Wash the apples and dry well with a piece of absorbent kitchen paper. Remove the cores, then cut into small chunks and put into a medium-sized mixing bowl.

Cut the celery into medium dice and add to the apples. Chop the walnuts finely, then mix in with the raisins. Toss well in the mayonnaise or the Old-Fashioned Dressing and cream. Transfer to a plastic container, cover and refrigerate until needed.

Serves 4

Recipes for the following salads can be found in other parts of the book:

Cold Beef Salad (p. 207), Ham Salad (p. 212),
Summer Salad (p. 218), Boiled Salad (p. 222),
Cucumber Salad (p. 224), Beetroot Salad (p. 212).

9

ICE-CREAMS, SOUFFLÉS AND COLD DESSERTS

'Picnic, indeed! You'll go to no picnic today, Anne Shirley! That shall be your punishment. And it isn't half severe enough for what you've done!'

'Not go to the picnic!' Anne sprang to her feet and clutched Marilla's hand. 'But you *promised* me I might! Oh, Marilla, I must go to the picnic. That was why I confessed. Punish me any way you like but that. Oh, Marilla, please, please let me go to the picnic. Think of the ice-cream! For anything you know I may never have a chance to taste ice-cream again.'

from *Anne of Green Gables*

North American picnics have featured ice-cream for some time but on this side of the Atlantic it has, until quite recently, rarely ventured outdoors. Now, with the latest wide-necked Thermos flasks, it can travel anywhere and remain in its frozen state for up to six hours.

For those whose picnic preparations leave them short of time and energy, a special section has been included on quick desserts.

Cold Dessert Tips

****** *To pack ice-cream:* fill a wide-necked Thermos with ice-cubes or crushed ice, close and leave for about 15 minutes.

Empty and dry well with absorbent kitchen paper. Spoon in the ice-cream (in large sections, if possible) and pack down firmly. Close tightly and pack. (Packing the Thermos amongst the ice-packs will keep it frozen even longer.) If the ice-cream is too hard to spoon out straight from the freezer, leave it in the refrigerator for a short time to soften up slightly.

****** To save plates, bring along a large serving spoon and scoop the ice-cream out into individual cones.

****** Once the ice-cream has melted, don't try to refreeze it. You'll have to throw it away as it may carry harmful bacteria.

****** If you want to serve cream with a dessert but haven't the space or the right container for it, whisk it up until thick, then spread a thin layer of it over the top of the dessert. Cover with foil or cling film and pack.

****** Small ramekin dishes are ideal for cold soufflés. They make serving easy and once covered with cling film can be stacked one on top of each other in the basket.

Ice-Creams

BUTTER PECAN ICE-CREAM
A traditional American ice-cream that is everyone's favourite.

2oz–4oz (50g–100g) pecan nuts	2 large eggs
1oz (25g) butter	1oz (25g) butter
salt	8oz (225ml) milk
7oz (200g) soft brown sugar	1 teaspoon vanilla
4oz (100ml) water	1 tablespoon sherry
large pinch of salt	½ pint (275ml) double cream

Melt 1oz (25g) of butter in a frying pan. Add the pecans and stir until well coated with the butter. Sprinkle generously with salt, then transfer to a baking tray. Put under a preheated grill (about 6″/15cm from it) and toast until well browned, turning frequently. Watch like a hawk as they can burn very easily. Turn out on to a plate or piece of foil, then put to one side. When cool, chop finely.

Put the sugar, water and salt into a heavy saucepan and heat gently until the sugar has dissolved. Crack the eggs into a basin and beat well. Then fit the basin into the top of a saucepan filled with several inches of water and put over moderate heat. Pour in the sugar syrup and beat over the hot water with an electric whisk until the mixture is very thick (it should leave a trail when the whisk is lifted out). Take off the heat and blend in the butter, milk, vanilla and sherry. Leave to cool, then whisk the cream until just thick and fold in. Pour into a plastic container and cover with a lid. Freeze until there is an inch (2·5cm) of frozen ice-cream around the sides of the container. Take out of the freezer and beat again until smooth, then add the chopped pecans and freeze until firm. Pack in an ice-cold wide-necked Thermos.

Serves 6–8

CREAMY LIME SORBET

3 ripe limes	6oz (175g) sugar
8oz (225ml) milk	2 large egg whites
½ pint (275ml) single cream	few drops green food colouring

Wipe the skins of the limes and grate finely, avoiding the white pith. Squeeze and strain all the juice.

Put the milk and sugar into a large bowl with the grated rind and juice. Stir until the sugar has completely dissolved, then blend in the cream and a few drops of green food colouring.

Whisk the egg whites until stiff. Pour the lime mixture in

slowly, folding in with a metal spoon. When completely blended, pour into a plastic container, cover with a lid and freeze until firm. (There is no need to beat again during the freezing.)

Serves 8

Quick Ice-Creams

BLACKBERRY AND LEMON ICE-CREAM

6oz (175g) sugar
4oz (100ml) water
8oz (225g) blackberries (fresh or frozen)

1 lemon
½ pint (275ml) double cream

Put the sugar and water into a saucepan and heat gently until the sugar has dissolved, stirring occasionally. Add the blackberries (if using frozen ones, thaw completely first) and cook until thick and pulpy. Take off the heat and leave to cool.

Squeeze and strain all the lemon juice and add to the blackberries. Whisk the cream until just thick and fold in lightly. Pour into a plastic container, cover with a lid and freeze until firm.

Serves 6–8

ORANGE PINEAPPLE ICE-CREAM

1 (14oz/400g) tin crushed pineapple
4oz (100ml) frozen orange juice (¾ of a regular tin)

6oz (175ml) sweetened condensed milk (¾ of a large tin)
½ pint (275ml) double cream

Put the crushed pineapple into a small saucepan with the orange juice and simmer over gentle heat until thick and syrupy. Put to one side to cool.

Whisk the cream until thick but not stiff, then fold in the cooled pineapple mixture and the condensed milk. When well blended, pour into a plastic container, cover with a lid and freeze until firm (no further beating required).

Serves 6–8

Cold Soufflés

ORANGE SOUFFLE WITH GRAND MARNIER

7 tablespoons concentrated
  orange juice
½oz (15g) gelatine
3 large eggs

4oz (100g) caster sugar
1 miniature bottle of Grand
  Marnier
½ pint (275ml) double cream

6–8 ramekin dishes or a 6″ (15cm) soufflé dish

In a small cup put 1 tablespoon of orange juice concentrate and 4 tablespoons of water. Sprinkle the gelatine on top and leave for about 5 minutes to soak. Then put the cup in a saucepan with a small amount of simmering water and leave until the gelatine has dissolved completely. Take the cup out and leave to cool to lukewarm.

Separate the eggs and put the yolks, sugar and the remaining orange juice concentrate in a medium basin. Whisk until well blended, then put over a saucepan of hot water and beat until thick and lemon-coloured (when the whisk is lifted out, the mixture should leave a trail behind).

When the egg mixture is thick, add the Grand Marnier and blend in well. Take the basin off the heat, pour in the gelatine in a steady stream and whisk in well. Rest the basin in a pan

163

filled with ice-cubes and stir until the mixture begins to thicken (or cool in the refrigerator, stirring from time to time). Then fold in the cream, whisked until just thick. Whisk the egg whites until stiff and fold in. Pour into individual ramekin dishes or a soufflé dish. Refrigerate until set, then spread with a thin layer of whipped cream (or leave as is). Keep in a cool place until needed, then cover with cling film and pack.

Serves 6–8

ICED RASPBERRY SOUFFLE

3 large eggs
2oz (50g) caster sugar
½ pint (275ml) milk
½oz (15g) gelatine

3 tablespoons water
1 tablespoon lemon juice
8oz (225g) raspberries
   + caster sugar to sweeten

¼ pint (150ml) double cream

6–8 ramekin dishes or a small (6″/15cm) soufflé dish

Separate the eggs and put the yolks with the caster sugar into a bowl. Blend together well. Pour the milk into a saucepan and heat to scalding point, then add gradually to the egg yolks and sugar. Pour the mixture back into the saucepan and stir over gentle heat until thick enough to coat a spoon. Take off the heat, cover with dampened greaseproof paper and leave to cool.

Put the water and lemon juice into a small cup and sprinkle the gelatine on top. Leave to soak for 5 minutes. Then put the cup in a small amount of hot water and leave until the gelatine has completely dissolved. Take out and cool to lukewarm.

- Put the raspberries in a bowl and sweeten to taste with caster sugar. Purée in a blender or put through a sieve. Whisk the cooled custard until completely smooth, then fold in the raspberry purée. Pour in the lukewarm gelatine in a steady stream and blend in well. Put the bowl in a pan filled with ice-cubes and stir until the mixture starts to thicken (or put into the refrigerator and stir from time to time until on the verge of setting). Whisk the cream until just thick and fold in. Then whisk the egg whites until stiff and fold in lightly. Pour into the ramekins or soufflé dish and chill until set. Decorate with cream (or leave as is), cover with cling film or foil and pack. Serve with icebox biscuits or jumbles.

Serves 6–8

QUICK LEMON SOUFFLE

This feather-light soufflé takes very little time to make and is perfect for hot summer picnics.

2 medium lemons	3 large eggs
½oz (15g) gelatine	2½oz (65g) caster sugar

Small soufflé dish, 4–6 ramekin dishes or plastic glasses

Grate the rind of the two lemons, then squeeze and strain all the juice. Put 4 tablespoons of the juice into a small cup and sprinkle the gelatine on top. Leave to soak for 5 minutes, then dissolve over hot water. Cool to lukewarm.

Separate the eggs, then beat the yolks with the sugar until thick and lemon-coloured. Gradually stir in the remaining lemon juice and rind. Pour in the gelatine in a steady stream and mix in well. Whisk the egg whites until stiff (but not dry) and fold in. When well blended, pour into ramekin dishes, glasses or soufflé dish. Chill until set. Cover with cling film and pack, if possible, near the ice-packs in the picnic basket.

Serves 4–6

COFFEE CHARLOTTE

2 packets of sponge fingers	½ pint (275ml) milk
1 tablespoon instant coffee	4 large eggs
1 teaspoon sugar	3oz (75g) caster sugar
1 tablespoon brandy or sherry	1 tablespoon brandy or sherry
5oz (150ml) boiling water	½oz (15g) gelatine
2 tablespoons instant coffee	½ pint (275ml) double cream

Charlotte mould or deep 6″ (15cm) cake tin

Put 1 teaspoon of sugar and a tablespoon of instant coffee into a small bowl. Pour in the boiling water and stir until the sugar has dissolved. Add the brandy and pour about a third of the mixture on to a large saucer. Lightly grease or oil the base of a charlotte mould or cake tin and line with a circle of grease-proof paper, then grease again. Dip the sponge fingers, one by one, into the coffee liquid (adding more when necessary) and use to line the base and sides of the tin (some will have to be trimmed to fit the tin).

Put 2 tablespoons of instant coffee into a small saucepan with the milk. Bring to scalding point, then take off the heat, cover and leave to infuse for 15 minutes. Separate the eggs and put the yolks and sugar into a basin over hot water. Whisk slightly to mix, then stir in the brandy and infused milk. Leave over gently simmering water, stirring frequently, until the mixture thickens enough to coat the back of a spoon. While it thickens, measure the remaining coffee liquid (used with the biscuits) into a small cup and make, if necessary, up to 4 tablespoons with water. Sprinkle the gelatine on top, and leave to soak for 5 minutes. Then put the cup in a small amount of hot water until the gelatine has completely dissolved. Cool to lukewarm, then pour into the thickened custard in a steady stream and mix in well. Take off the heat and put the basin into a bowl or pan of ice-cubes. Stir until the mixture begins to set. Whisk the cream until just thick and fold in. Whisk the egg whites until stiff and fold in gently. Pour into lined charlotte mould and chill until set. Cover the tin with foil or cling film and pack. Reverse out on to a plate just before serving. Serve with cream or on its own.

Serves 8–10

Cold Desserts

SNOW PUDDING

½oz (15g) gelatine
2oz (50ml) cold water
8oz (225ml) boiling water

6oz (175g) sugar
juice and rind of 2 large lemons
2 large egg whites

6–8 glasses, ramekins or a small soufflé dish

Put the cold water into a small cup and sprinkle the gelatine on top. Leave to soak for 5 minutes. Then put the cup over or in a small amount of hot water until the gelatine has completely dissolved.

Grate the rind of both lemons and squeeze all the juice. Strain into a large mixing bowl. Add the sugar, lemon rind and boiling water. Stir until the sugar has completely dissolved, then add, in a steady stream, the gelatine. Mix in well, then leave in a cool place (stirring occasionally) until it is just beginning to set. Whisk until frothy and very white in colour. Whisk the egg whites until stiff and fold in lightly.

Pour the mixture into a small soufflé dish, ramekins or glasses. Chill for several hours, then cover with cling film or foil and pack. Serve with pouring custard and biscuits or cake.

Serves 6–8

CREME CARAMEL

This recipe, unlike the traditional 'crème renversée', puts the caramel *into* the custard rather than over and is much more practical for a picnic.

4oz (100g) caster sugar
5oz (150ml) water
4 large eggs

1oz (25g) caster sugar
¾ pint (425ml) milk
few drops of vanilla essence

6 ramekin dishes
Preheat oven to 325°F / Gas Mark 3 / 170°C.

Put the sugar and half the water in a large heavy saucepan and heat gently until the sugar has dissolved. Then bring to the boil and boil rapidly until it turns a rich caramel colour. Pour in the remaining water (cover pouring hand and stand back as this may splatter) and stir until completely blended. Then take off the heat and put to one side to cool.

Pour the milk into a small saucepan, scald and mix into the cooled caramel. Beat the eggs, sugar and vanilla essence together until light, then add the caramel milk. Mix well and strain into a jug. Divide the mixture equally between the ramekin dishes and place these in a small roasting tin filled with an inch (2·5cm) of warm water. Bake in the centre of the oven for about an hour, or until firm. Take the dishes out and leave to cool. Then cover with cling film or foil and pack. Just before serving, loosen round the edges with a knife and reverse out on to individual plates.

Serves 6

LEMON PUDDING

1 large ripe lemon
1oz (25g) plain flour
7oz (200g) caster sugar

¼ teaspoon salt
2 large eggs, separated
8oz (225ml) milk

Lightly grease 6 ramekin dishes.
Preheat oven to 350°F / Gas Mark 4 / 180°C.

Grate all the lemon rind (being careful to take only the yellow part), then squeeze and strain all the juice. Put to one side. Sift the flour, sugar and salt together into a large mixing bowl.

Beat the egg yolks until thick and lemon-coloured, then blend in the lemon juice and milk. Make a well in the dry ingredients and gradually stir in the egg mixture with the lemon rind.

Whisk the egg whites until stiff, then lightly fold into the batter. Pour into the ramekin dishes (filling almost to the top) and stand in a roasting tin filled with about an inch (2·5cm) of warm water. Bake in the centre of preheated oven for 50 minutes or until lightly browned and firm to the touch. Take out, dust lightly with caster sugar, cover with foil and pack in an insulated bag. (Or leave to cool, then cover with foil or cling film and pack.)

Serves 6

APPLE BROWN BETTY

¾lb (350g) cooking apples
3oz (75g) fresh breadcrumbs
5oz (150g) brown sugar
½ teaspoon ground cinnamon

½ teaspoon ground nutmeg
¼ teaspoon ground cloves
2oz (50g) butter
2oz (50ml) lemon juice

5oz (150ml) water

6–8 ramekin dishes
Preheat oven to 350°F / Gas Mark 4 / 180°C.

Peel, core and chop the apples into small chunks. Put in a bowl with the fresh breadcrumbs, brown sugar and spices, mixing well. Melt the butter and blend into the mixture with the lemon juice. Then divide equally amongst the ramekin dishes and pour a small amount of water over each one. Cover with foil and bake in the oven for 20 minutes, then remove the foil and bake for a further 20 minutes.

To serve warm, pack at once (covering with foil first) in an insulated bag or in any of the ways suggested in the introductory section on Keeping Food Hot. Or leave to cool, then cover with cling film or foil and pack. Serve either way with fresh cream.

Serves 6–8

Quick Desserts

CIDER SYLLABUB

4oz (100ml) dry cider
1 tablespoon brandy or sherry
peel of 1 large lemon
juice of ½ large lemon
3oz–4oz (75g–100g) sugar

½ teaspoon grated nutmeg
½ teaspoon ground cinnamon
½ pint (275ml) double cream
cinnamon and nutmeg to
  decorate

Ramekin dishes or glasses

Put the cider, brandy (or sherry) and lemon juice into a bowl with the lemon peel (pared off the lemon in strips). Cover with a plate or cling film and leave for a few hours or overnight.

Strain the mixture into a large bowl and stir in the sugar, cinnamon and nutmeg. Stir until the sugar has completely dissolved, then pour in the cream (from a height if possible), blending in with a fork. Then whisk until the mixture is thick enough to hold its shape. Spoon into ramekin dishes or glasses and sprinkle lightly with cinnamon and nutmeg. Cover with cling film and refrigerate until ready to pack.

Serves 4–6

CHOCOLATE MOUSSE

3oz (75g) plain chocolate   ½ pint (275ml) double cream
1oz (25g) caster sugar   4 large egg whites

6 ramekin dishes or plastic glasses

Put the chocolate on a plate or in a bowl over (not in) hot water. Leave to melt, then take off the heat. Blend well with a spatula or palette knife, then cool slightly.

Whisk the cream until thick, then fold in the sugar and cooled chocolate. Whisk the egg whites until stiff and fold in lightly. When well blended, spoon into ramekin dishes or glasses. Chill until set, then cover with cling film and pack. (Add a small dollop of whipped cream to each dish before covering, if you like.)

Serves 6

CARIBBEAN GRAPE DESSERT

1lb (450g) green grapes   4–5 tablespoons soft brown
1lb (450g) black grapes   sugar
3–4 tablespoons light rum   5oz (150g) plain yogurt
        ½ pint (275ml) double cream

6–8 ramekin dishes or plastic glasses

Wash and dry the grapes well. Cut in half lengthwise and remove the pips. Put into a medium mixing bowl. In another bowl, put the yogurt, rum and brown sugar, stirring until the sugar has completely dissolved. In a third bowl, whisk the cream until thick. Fold the yogurt mixture into the cream, then gently blend in the grapes. Spoon into glasses or ramekin dishes and refrigerate until well chilled. Then cover with cling film and pack (keeping chilled if possible). This must be made the day of the picnic.

Serves 6–8

BUTTERSCOTCH CREAM

4oz (100g) soft brown sugar   4oz (100ml) hot water
1½oz (40g) butter   8oz (225g) thick custard
½ pint (275ml) double cream

6–8 ramekin dishes or plastic glasses

Melt the brown sugar and butter together in a large heavy saucepan over low heat. When completely melted, add the hot water and stir until well blended. Bring to the boil, then reduce the heat and simmer until thick and syrupy. Put to one side to cool slightly.

Mix the custard with the caramel mixture, then whisk the cream until thick and fold in. Spoon into ramekins or glasses and refrigerate until needed. Just before packing, decorate the tops with crushed butterscotch, 'hundreds and thousands' or a dollop of whipped cream, then cover with cling film.

Serves 4–6

APRICOT AMBER

1 (14oz/400g) tin apricots   ½ pint (275ml) thick custard
few drops of vanilla essence   (tinned or home-made)
1 teaspoon lemon juice   2 large egg whites
4oz (100g) caster sugar

6–8 ramekin dishes
Preheat oven to 350°F / Gas Mark 4 / 180°C.

Drain the apricots and purée in a blender or put through a sieve until smooth. Put into a bowl and mix in the vanilla essence, lemon juice and custard. Divide the mixture between the ramekins, filling almost to the top of each one. Whisk the egg whites until stiff, then whisk in half the sugar, a tablespoonful at a time. Fold in the remainder with a spatula. Cover the top of each ramekin with meringue, making sure that it covers all the edges to seal completely. Bake in the centre of preheated oven for 15–20 minutes or until the meringue is golden brown. Pack at once on the top layer of the basket or leave to cool.

Serves 6–8

BLACKBERRY MOUSSE

1 (10oz/275g) tin blackberries
2½ tablespoons sugar
  (or to taste)
¼ pint (150ml) double cream
½ pint (275ml) thick custard
  (tinned or home-made)
juice of ½ lemon

4–6 ramekin dishes or plastic glasses

Purée the blackberries in a blender or put through a sieve until smooth. Add the sugar and lemon juice and stir until the sugar has dissolved. Put the custard in a bowl, then whisk the cream until thick and fold in. Blend in the purée gradually. Check for sweetness and add more sugar if necessary. Spoon or pour into ramekins or glasses. Chill until needed, then cover with cling film and pack.

Serves 4–6

Recipes for the following desserts can be found in other parts of the book:

Strawberries and Peaches Romanoff (p. 257)
Crème Bûlée (p. 241), Sussex Whips (p. 213), Fruit Salad (p. 269)

10

PASTRIES, CAKES AND BISCUITS

Manmade improvements on Nature at the Picnic
Grounds consisted of several circles of flat stones to
serve as fireplaces and a wooden privy in the shape of a
Japanese pagoda. The creek at the close of the summer
ran sluggishly through long grass, now and then almost
disappearing to reappear as a shallow pool. Lunch had
been set out on large white tablecloths close by, shaded
from the heat of the sun by two or three spreading
gums. In addition to the chicken pie, angel cake, jellies
and the tepid bananas inseparable from an Australian
picnic, Cook had provided a handsome iced cake in the
shape of a heart . . .

from *Picnic at Hanging Rock*

This chapter provides a good excuse to raid Continental, American and Australian picnic baskets. There's nothing that perks
up a meal outdoors like a slice of rich banana cake, a handful
of chocolate brownies or a wedge of French apricot flan . . .

Pastry, Cake and Biscuit Tips

****** *To pack large cakes:* put the cake on a plate and fit
inside a cake tin which has been lined with a double square of
absorbent kitchen paper (this keeps it from slipping). Cover with
the lid and pack.

****** *To pack pies*: if a double crust pie or one in which the filling has been cooked with the pastry, leave in the pie plate, cover with a loose 'hood' of foil and pack on the top layer of the basket. For pies which have the filling added to a pre-baked pastry shell, slide the pastry after cooling on to a loose flan base or plate. Fill, then cover with a loose 'hood' of foil and pack. If the pie has a glaze, put it (on its tin base) into a cake tin lined with a double square of absorbent kitchen paper, wedge it well to keep from slipping and cover with a lid.

****** It's a good idea when baking pastry blind for picnic pies and flans, to bake it for a few minutes longer than you normally would. This keeps it crisper and less affected by a moist filling.

****** All the recipes for pies and flans in this chapter can be made into tartlets instead if you prefer. These are extremely practical for, as well as being easy to eat, any that are not used can be frozen for another time.

Pastry

PLAIN SHORTCRUST PASTRY

8oz (225g) plain flour
4oz–6oz (100g–175g) butter,
   margarine or lard
   (or a mixture of any two)

4 tablespoons iced water
large pinch of salt

Sift the flour with a pinch of salt into a mixing bowl. Cut the fat in with two knives and when the pieces are well coated with flour, rub in with fingertips until the mixture resembles bread-crumbs. Tip in the iced water, reserving about a tablespoon, and mix quickly with a knife (if it seems dry, add the last tablespoon of water). Press into a ball with fingers and knead lightly until smooth. Put into a polythene bag and chill for 20–30 minutes before baking.

RICH SHORTCRUST PASTRY I

8oz (225g) plain flour
large pinch of salt
6oz (175g) butter
or 4oz (100g) butter and
2oz (50g) lard or margarine

2 tablespoons caster sugar
1 standard egg yolk
3-4 tablespoons iced water

Sift the flour with a pinch of salt into a mixing bowl. Cut in the fat with two knives and when well coated with the flour, rub in with fingertips until the mixture resembles breadcrumbs. Blend in sugar. Tip in the egg yolk mixed with 3 tablespoons of water and mix quickly with a knife (adding another tablespoon of water if the dough seems dry). Press with fingers into a ball and knead lightly until smooth. Put into a polythene bag and chill for 30 minutes before using.

RICH PASTRY II

8oz (225g) plain flour
large pinch of salt
4oz (100g) butter

2oz (50g) caster or icing sugar
2 standard egg yolks
2-3 tablespoons iced water

Sift the flour and salt into a mixing bowl. Cut in the fat with two knives and, when well coated with the flour, rub in with fingertips until the mixture resembles breadcrumbs. Blend in sugar. Mix the yolks with 2 tablespoons of the iced water, sprinkle over the mixture and blend in quickly with a fork or knife (adding more water if it seems dry). Shape into a ball and knead lightly until smooth. Put into a polythene bag and chill for 30 minutes before using.

FRENCH FLAN PASTRY (Pâté Sucrée)

6oz (175g) plain flour
pinch of salt
3oz (75g) butter, at room
  temperature

2oz (50g) caster sugar
2 standard egg yolks
a drop of vanilla essence

176

Sift the flour and salt on to a clean counter or marble slab. Make a well in the centre and in it put the two egg yolks, sugar, vanilla essence and butter. Using the fingertips of one hand, mix these ingredients together until they form a soft paste. Then with fingers or the edge of a palette knife, draw in the flour gradually from around the sides. Shape into a ball and chill in a polythene bag for 30 minutes before using.

ALMOND PASTRY

6oz (175g) plain flour
pinch salt
4oz (100g) butter
2oz (50g) ground almonds

2oz (50g) caster sugar
1 large egg yolk
drop of vanilla essence
1–2 tablespoons iced water

Sift the flour and salt into a mixing bowl. Cut the butter in with two knives and, when well coated with the flour, rub in with fingertips until the mixture resembles breadcrumbs. Blend in the sugar and ground almonds. Mix the yolk with 1 tablespoon of water and tip in, mixing quickly with a fork or knife (adding more water if the mixture seems dry). Shape into a ball and knead lightly until smooth. Put into a polythene bag and chill for 30 minutes before using.

AMERICAN PASTRY

10oz (275g) plain flour
½ teaspoon salt
4oz (100g) lard

2oz (50g) butter
6 tablespoons iced water

Sift the flour and salt into a mixing bowl. Cut in the fat with two knives, then rub in with fingertips until the mixture resembles coarse breadcrumbs. Sprinkle the iced water over the top and mix in quickly with a fork. Shape the pastry into a ball, then knead lightly until smooth. Chill in a polythene bag for 30 minutes before using.

Pies, Flans and Tarts

BLACKCURRANT PIE

For those who envisage blackcurrant stains all over the best picnic tablecloth, fear not. The filling in this pie is very thick and should stay comfortably on the plate, unless placed at a precarious angle on knees or laps.

10oz (275g) rich shortcrust pastry

2 (6oz/184g) tins of black-currants

2 tablespoons lemon juice

4oz (100g) sugar

3 tablespoons flour

beaten egg to glaze

8½″ (21·5cm) pie plate or dish

Empty the tins of blackcurrants into a medium saucepan. Stir in the lemon juice and sugar. Put the flour in a small cup and slowly pour in enough of the blackcurrant juice to make a smooth, runny paste. Then tip this mixture into the saucepan with the other ingredients. Heat gently until boiling (stirring occasionally), then reduce the heat and simmer until thick. Take off the heat and leave to cool slightly.

Take just over half the pastry, roll out and use to line the pie plate. Trim the edges and dampen slightly with cold water. Pour in the blackcurrant mixture and spread out evenly. Then roll out the remaining pastry and cover the pie. Cut off any surplus, then pinch the edges together, knock up and flute. Decorate the top with any pastry trimmings and cut a small hole or a few slits in the top to let the steam escape. Brush lightly with milk and bake in the centre of the oven (preheated to 425°F / Gas Mark 7 / 220°C) for 30–40 minutes or until nicely browned. Take out and dust lightly with caster sugar. To serve warm, cover with foil and pack at once in an insulated bag. Otherwise, leave to cool, then cover with foil and pack carefully (making sure it is kept level) in the picnic basket. Pack a large knife and a pie or fish slice to serve with. Serve with cream or on its own.

Serves 8

LEMON MERINGUE PIE

Check before you make this that you have a cake tin big enough to transport the pie in. Otherwise you might end up holding it on your lap for the entire journey.

6oz (175g) rich shortcrust pastry

Filling: 2 large egg yolks
2 large ripe lemons
2oz (50g) cornflour   *Meringue:*
7oz (200g) caster sugar   2 large egg whites
½ pint (275ml) water   4oz (100g) caster sugar

8″ (20cm) flan ring or tin (or pie dish)
Preheat oven to 375°F / Gas Mark 5 / 190°C.

Roll out the pastry thinly and use to line the flan ring or pie dish. Trim the edges, then prick the base lightly with a fork. Cover the base and sides with a circle of greaseproof paper and fill with baking beans. Bake in the centre of the oven for 15 minutes, removing the paper and beans for the last 5 minutes. Take out and put to one side.

While the pastry is in the oven, grate the lemon rind finely, then squeeze and strain all the juice. Put the sugar, cornflour and lemon rind into a small saucepan and gradually stir in the water. Put over gentle heat and bring to the boil, stirring constantly. Boil for 2–3 minutes or until very thick, then take off the heat and beat in the egg yolks with a whisk or wooden spoon. Pour into the pastry case and level off with the back of a spoon. Whisk the egg whites until stiff, then whisk in half the sugar,

1 tablespoon at a time. Fold in the remainder and pile on top of the lemon filling, making sure that all the edges are sealed.

Lower the oven temperature to 300°F / Gas Mark 2 / 150°C and bake until the meringue is crisp and lightly browned. Take out and cool away from draughts. Line the bottom of a round cake tin with a double layer of absorbent kitchen paper or a tea towel and place the pie dish carefully on top. Put the lid on and pack the tin in the basket, wedging it so that it remains level. Take a sharp knife and a pie or fish slice to serve with.

Serves 8

FOUR SEASONS FLAN

8oz (225g) rich shortcrust
pastry
1 large orange
8oz (225g) blackberries*

8oz (225g) strawberries*
4oz (100g) green grapes
½ pint (275ml) double cream
1 tablespoon caster sugar

Glaze:
4 tablespoons apricot jam
4 tablespoons redcurrant jelly

3 tablespoons lemon juice

10″ (25cm) fluted ceramic flan dish
Preheat oven to 375°F / Gas Mark 5 / 190°C.

Roll out the pastry and use to line the flan dish. Trim off any surplus and prick the base lightly with a fork. Cover the base and sides with a large circle of greaseproof paper and fill with baking beans. Bake in the centre of a preheated oven for 15 minutes, then remove the paper and beans and bake for a further 10–12 minutes. Leave to cool completely.

Peel the orange and separate into segments, removing the thin membranes and white pith. Rinse the blackberries and strawberries and leave in a colander to drain. Wash the grapes and

* Fresh berries are best for this recipe, but if unavailable use frozen ones (making sure they are completely thawed and well drained first).

dry well in absorbent kitchen paper. Halve and remove the pips.

Whisk the cream and sugar together until thick. Reserve about 2 tablespoons for decoration, then spread the rest evenly over the base of the cooled flan case. Mark with a knife into four equal triangles. Arrange a different kind of fruit in each triangle, working from the outside to the centre. Put the apricot jam and redcurrant jelly into separate saucepans and add 1½ tablespoons of lemon juice to each one. Stir over low heat until thick and syrupy. Strain, then brush or spoon the apricot glaze over the grapes and oranges and the redcurrant glaze over the berries. Chill until set, then put a dollop of whipped cream in the centre. Cover with a loose 'hood' of foil and pack carefully on the top layer of the basket. (Make sure it is resting on something level so that it doesn't slide.)

Serves 8–10

FRENCH APRICOT FLAN

6oz (175g) almond or French flan pastry

2 (14oz/400g) tins of apricots
¼ pint (150ml) thick custard
few drops of vanilla essence

Glaze:
4–5 tablespoons apricot jam   juice of half a lemon

8″ (20cm) flan ring or tin
Preheat oven to 375°F / Gas Mark 5 / 190°C.

Roll out the pastry thinly and use to line the flan tin. Trim off any surplus and prick the base lightly with a fork. Cover the base and sides with a circle of crumpled greaseproof paper, then fill with baking beans. Bake in the centre of a preheated oven for 12 minutes, then remove the beans and paper and bake for a further 8–10 minutes. Take out and cool completely, then slide on to a loose flan base.

Mix the **vanilla into** the custard and spread a thin layer over the base of the pastry case (you may not need the full quantity). Pour the juice off the apricots and drain well on absorbent kitchen paper. Then arrange the fruit on top of the custard in concentric circles, working from the outside into the centre.

Measure the apricot jam and lemon juice into a saucepan and heat gently until thick and syrupy, stirring constantly. Strain, then brush or spoon, while still warm, over the apricots. Leave in a cool place until set. To pack: leave the flan on the tin base and put back carefully into its fluted tin, a slightly larger flan dish or a cake tin with a removable base. Cover with a loose 'hood' of foil and pack. (The pastry case can be made the day before but should not be filled until a few hours before leaving for the picnic.)

Serves 8

APPLE AND MINCEMEAT PIES

10oz (275g) plain or rich short-crust pastry

1 large cooking apple (about 8oz/ 225g in weight)

12oz (350g) mincemeat
½ lemon
2–3 tablespoons caster sugar

Patty tins
Preheat oven to 400°F / Gas Mark 6 / 200°C.

Peel the apple, core and cut into small chunks. Put into a small bowl and sprinkle with the juice of half a lemon. Add 2–3 tablespoons of sugar (this depends on the tartness of the fruit) and mix well. Blend in the mincemeat.

Roll out two-thirds of the pastry and cut out 12 circles slightly larger than the patty tins. Line the tins with the pastry, then fill each one with a dollop of the apple/mincemeat mixture, piling it up slightly in the centre. Roll out the remaining dough and cut out 12 circles for lids. Dampen the edges of the pastry cases with water, then put on the lids, pinching the edges together to seal. Cut a few slits in the top of each one to let the steam escape, then brush with water or milk and sprinkle with caster sugar. Bake for about 30 minutes or until golden brown. Take carefully out of the tins and wrap each one in foil (if serving hot) and pack in an insulated bag. Or leave to cool and pack in a tin or plastic container.

Makes 12 small pies

BUTTER TARTS

6oz (175g) rich shortcrust pastry

Filling:

3oz (75g) currants or raisins	1 egg
1oz (25g) butter, at room temperature	4oz (100ml) golden syrup
	½ teaspoon vanilla
2oz (50g) soft brown sugar	½ teaspoon lemon juice

Patty tins
Preheat oven to 375°F / Gas Mark 5 / 190°C.

Roll the pastry out thinly and cut out (with fluted cutter, if possible) 12 circles to fit the patty tins. Line the tins with the pastry, then chill until the filling is ready.

Put the raisins in a bowl and pour over enough boiling water to cover them. Leave for 15 minutes, then drain. Soften the butter in a bowl, then add the sugar and cream together until light and fluffy. Beat the egg lightly and blend in with the golden syrup, vanilla, lemon juice and raisins.

Put spoonfuls of the mixture into the pastry-lined tins (be careful not to over-fill). Bake for 15–20 minutes or until the pastry is golden brown (if the filling starts to bubble, turn the heat down slightly). Leave in the tins for several minutes, then lift out on to a wire rack and cool. Pack in a tin or plastic container, separating each layer with greaseproof paper or foil.

Makes 12 small tarts

Cakes

BANANA CAKE

This makes a very light, moist double layer cake, large enough to serve 10–12 people.

4oz (100g) butter, at room
   temperature
12oz (350g) sugar
2 large eggs
large pinch of salt
8oz (225g) plain flour

2 teaspoons baking powder
4oz (100ml) milk
½ teaspoon vanilla
2oz–4oz (50g–100g) finely
   chopped walnuts
3 medium bananas (ripe)

1 teaspoon bicarbonate of soda

Grease and dust with flour two 8″ (20cm) sandwich tins (they must be at least 1″/2·5cm deep).
Preheat oven to 350°F / Gas Mark 4 / 180°C.

Soften the butter in a large mixing bowl. Add the sugar (sift first) and cream together until light and fluffy. Beat the eggs lightly, then blend in gradually.

Sift the flour, salt and baking powder together several times and then on to a plate or sheet of greaseproof paper. Add to the creamed mixture alternately with the milk, beating well after each addition.

Mash the bananas to a pulp (a potato masher is ideal for this) and stir in the bicarbonate of soda. Then fold them, with the chopped walnuts and vanilla, into the batter. Pour into prepared tins and level off the tops with the back of a spoon. Bake in the centre of preheated oven for 30–40 minutes or until a toothpick inserted in the centre comes out clean. Take out of the oven and leave in the tins for 5–10 minutes. Then loosen round the edges with a knife and carefully reverse out on to a wire rack. Then slide on to a plate or loose flan base.

Butter Icing:

2oz (50g) butter

8oz–10oz (225g–275g) sifted
  icing sugar

1 large egg white

1 teaspoon lemon juice

Melt the butter, put into a small bowl and gradually beat in the icing sugar and lemon juice. Add just enough icing sugar for the mixture to hold its shape without making it too thick to spread. Then whisk the egg white until stiff and fold in. Use a round-bladed or palette knife to spread the icing on the bottom layer, then cover with the second layer and ice the top and sides of the cake. Put into a cake tin or cover with a loose 'hood' of foil and pack.

BLACK FOREST CAKE

2oz (50g) dark chocolate

2oz (50ml) water

3oz (75g) plain flour

3 large eggs

5oz (150g) caster sugar

large pinch of salt

Filling/Icing:

2oz (50g) sifted icing sugar

4oz (100g) grated dark
  chocolate

½ pint (275ml) double cream*

Grease a deep cake tin (3"/7·5cm deep and 6"/15cm in diameter). Line the base with a circle of greaseproof paper. Grease again and dust lightly with flour.

Preheat oven to 375°F / Gas Mark 5 / 190°C.

Grate the chocolate and put with the water into a small saucepan. Melt, without stirring, over low heat. Take off the heat, blend well with a palette knife and leave to cool slightly.

Sift the flour and salt into a mixing bowl. Put the eggs and sugar into a pudding basin and whisk over a saucepan of hot

* Black cherries and kirsch can be added to make it more authentic, but they tend to make the cake slightly soggy and not as practical for a picnic.

water until thick (the mixture should leave a trail when the whisk is lifted out). Take off the heat and lightly fold in the flour and melted chocolate. Pour into prepared tin and bake in the centre of the oven for about 45 minutes or until a toothpick inserted into the centre comes out clean. Cool on a wire rack.

Put the cake on a plate or loose flan base, then cut in half horizontally. Whisk the cream until thick and spread the bottom layer with half the quantity. Cover with the second layer and spread the remaining cream evenly over the top and sides. Divide the grated chocolate into two equal portions. Mix one half with the sifted icing sugar and using a palette knife press round the sides and top of the cake. Sprinkle half the remaining chocolate over the top of the cake and press the rest round the sides. Chill until needed. Then cover with a loose 'hood' of foil and pack on the top layer of the basket. Or put the cake (still on the plate) into a large cake tin, cover with a lid and pack.

Serves 8

ORANGE ROULADE

3oz (75g) plain flour
1 tablespoon cornflour
1½ teaspoons baking powder
large pinch of salt

4 large eggs
6oz (175g) caster sugar
1 tablespoon orange juice
½ teaspoon orange essence

Filling:
2 large egg whites
3oz (75g) caster sugar
¼ pint (150ml) double cream

grated rind of 1 orange
1 tablespoon caster sugar

Grease a swiss roll tin and line with greaseproof paper, then grease again.
Preheat oven to 350°F / Gas Mark 4 / 180°C.

Sift the flour, cornflour, baking powder and salt together several times. Then sift on to a plate or sheet of greaseproof paper.

Separate the eggs and put the yolks in a basin with 4oz (100g)

186

sugar, the orange juice and orange essence. Put the basin over a saucepan of hot water and whisk until thick and lemon-coloured (the mixture should leave a trail when the whisk is lifted out). Whisk the whites until stiff, then whisk in 1oz (25g) sugar, a tablespoonful at a time. Fold in the remainder, then lightly fold into the yolk mixture. Tip the flour on top and fold in very gently. Pour into the prepared tin and spread well into the corners and level off with the back of a spoon. Bake in the centre of the oven for 10–15 minutes or until well risen and golden (it should spring back lightly if touched with a finger). Turn out on to a sheet of greaseproof paper sprinkled with caster sugar. Remove the greaseproof paper backing and roll up tightly in the fresh paper. Then wrap in a tea towel and leave to cool.

Whisk the egg whites until stiff and the cream until just thick. Fold the first into the second with a tablespoon of caster sugar and the grated orange rind. Carefully unroll cooled cake and with a palette knife spread an even layer of the filling over it (keeping it about $\frac{1}{2}''$/1cm from the outside edges). Then roll up again carefully. Dust the cake with caster sugar and wrap in a piece of foil. Refrigerate until needed.

Serves 8-10

GINGERBREAD

7oz (200ml) treacle	8oz (225g) plain flour
3oz (75ml) golden syrup	1 teaspoon ground ginger
4oz (100g) butter, at room temperature	$\frac{1}{2}$ teaspoon mixed spice
	2 large eggs
4oz (100g) soft brown sugar	large pinch salt
$\frac{1}{2}$ teaspoon bicarbonate of soda	

Grease and lightly flour a deep 6″ (15cm) cake tin.
Preheat oven to 325°F / Gas Mark 3 / 170°C.

Put the treacle and golden syrup into a small saucepan and blend together over gentle heat. Then cool to lukewarm.

Soften the butter in a large mixing bowl, then add the sugar and cream with a wooden spoon until light and fluffy. Sift the flour and spices together on to a plate or sheet of greaseproof paper.

Add a pinch of salt to the eggs and beat lightly. Stir the bicarbonate of soda into the cooled syrup. Then blend the two together and add alternately with the flour to the creamed mixture. When thoroughly blended, pour into the prepared tin and level off with the back of a spoon. Bake in the centre of the oven for 1¼–1½ hours or until a toothpick inserted in the centre comes out clean. (If the top seems to be getting too brown, cover loosely with foil.) Loosen the edges with a knife, then reverse out on to a wire rack. Stand right side up and leave to cool. Pack and store in a polythene bag. Serve sliced, with butter, cheese or on its own.

Serves 8

INDIVIDUAL PEACH UPSIDE-DOWN CAKES

1 (15oz/425g) tin of sliced peaches
3oz (75g) caster sugar
1 teaspoon ground cinnamon
½ teaspoon mixed spice
2 level tablespoons flour

6oz (175g) plain flour
4oz (100g) sugar
1 teaspoon baking powder
¼ teaspoon salt
2 egg yolks
1oz (25g) butter, melted

5oz (150ml) milk

8 ramekin dishes, well greased
Preheat oven to 425°F / Gas Mark 7 / 220°C.

Drain the peaches and cut the slices very thinly. Divide equally amongst the ramekin dishes. Mix the caster sugar, cinnamon, mixed spice and flour together and sprinkle evenly over the peaches.

Sift the flour, sugar, baking powder and salt into a mixing

bowl. Beat the egg yolks until thick, then blend in the melted butter and milk. Make a well in the dry ingredients and gradually stir in the egg yolk mixture. Stir only until all the flour has been blended in, then pour over the peaches. Bake in the centre of the oven for about 30 minutes. Take out and leave in the ramekins for about 20 minutes. Then carefully reverse on to a wire rack (put a square of kitchen paper underneath to catch any excess syrup). Leave the dishes on for a further 10 minutes, then remove and leave the cakes to cool completely. Pack in a tin or a plastic container.

Makes 8 small cakes

QUICK LEMON CHEESECAKE
(using a blender)

Although this takes very little time to make, it does need 1–2 hours in a refrigerator to set and so can't really be made at the last minute.

6oz (175g) wheatmeal biscuits	½oz (15g) gelatine
3oz (75g) butter	2 large eggs
1oz (25g) caster sugar	4oz (100g) caster sugar
	8oz (225g) cottage cheese
1 large lemon	8oz (225g) cream cheese

¼ pint (150ml) double cream

8″ (20cm) spring-form tin or cake tin with a loose base

Grate the lemon rind, then squeeze and strain all the juice. Pour 4 tablespoons of the juice into a small cup and sprinkle the gelatine on top. Leave to soak for 5 minutes. Then put the cup in a small amount of simmering water and leave until the gelatine has completely dissolved. Put to one side and cool to lukewarm.

Put the biscuits into a strong polythene bag and crush to crumbs with a rolling pin. Melt the butter, then add the sugar and crumbs, mixing well. Press the mixture into the bottom of a spring-form cake tin, reserving one-third of the quantity for the top.

Separate the eggs, putting the yolks in the blender and the whites in a mixing bowl. Add the sugar, lemon rind, remaining juice and half the cottage cheese to the yolks and blend at low speed until smooth. Then gradually blend in the remaining cottage cheese and the cream cheese. Take the centre cap off the blender lid and, with the machine on low speed, pour in the gelatine in a steady stream. Blend until well mixed, then pour into a mixing bowl. Whisk the cream until thick and fold in. Whisk the egg whites with a pinch of salt until stiff and fold in gently. Pour the mixture into the cake tin and sprinkle with the remaining crumbs. Refrigerate until set (1–2 hours). To pack, leave the cheesecake in the tin, cover with foil and put on the top layer of the basket. Remove the tin just before serving (leaving it on the tin base so that it is easy to cut).

Serves 8

SURPRISE SPONGE CAKE (Quick)

4oz (100g) soft butter or
   margarine
4oz (100g) caster sugar

2 large eggs
1 teaspoon vanilla essence
4oz (100g) self-raising flour

Filling:
8oz (225g) raspberries
¼ pint (150ml) double cream
sugar to taste
caster or icing sugar to decorate

Grease a deep 6″ (15cm) round cake tin and dust lightly with flour.
Preheat oven to 350°F / Gas Mark 4 / 180°C

Soften the butter in a mixing bowl. Blend in the sugar gradually and cream until light and fluffy. Beat the eggs with the vanilla, then add to the creamed mixture alternately with the sifted flour. Beat with a wooden spoon until thoroughly blended, then pour into prepared tin. Bake in the centre of the oven for about 25 minutes or until firm to the touch. Reverse out on to a wire rack, turn right side up and leave to cool.

Put the raspberries in a bowl and add sugar to taste. Whisk the cream until thick, then lightly fold in the berries. When the cake is quite cold, turn it over and carefully cut out a deep circle from the base – about an inch (2·5cm) from the outside edge all around and as deep as the centre of the cake. Gently pull this centre portion out, loosening the base with a knife as you go. Fill the hole which is left with the raspberries and cream. Press the centre portion back in firmly and stand right side up. Dust with caster or icing sugar and pack in a cake tin or plastic container (or wrap in foil). When ready to serve, slice from the centre into triangles.

Serves 6

Biscuits

SHREWSBURY BISCUITS

4oz (100g) butter, at room temperature
4oz (100g) caster sugar
grated rind of 1 lemon
1 large egg
8oz (225g) plain flour
3oz (75g) currants

Lightly grease a baking tray.
Preheat oven to 350°F / Gas Mark 4 / 180°C.

Put the butter into a large mixing bowl and soften slightly with a wooden spoon. Add the sugar gradually and cream until light and fluffy. Beat the egg and blend in. Grate the lemon rind, sift the flour and add to the mixture with the currants. Turn the dough out on to a lightly floured counter and roll to a $\frac{1}{4}''$ (·50cm) thickness. Cut into rounds with a $2\frac{1}{2}''$ (6cm) or 2″ (5cm) fluted cutter and lift with a fish slice or palette knife on to the baking tray. Prick lightly with a fork and bake just above the centre of the oven for about 12 minutes or until the edges turn a light fawn colour. Lift on to a wire rack and dust with caster sugar. Pack in a tin or polythene bag.

Makes about 18 biscuits

JUMBLES

4oz (100g) butter, at room temperature
4oz (100g) caster sugar
1 large egg

7oz (200g) plain flour
icing sugar for decoration
caster sugar and flour for rolling out
1 tablespoon brandy or sherry

Grease a large baking tray.

Put the butter in a large mixing bowl and soften with a wooden spoon. Add the sugar and cream together until light and fluffy. Beat the egg well and blend into the creamed mixture with the brandy. Sift the flour and add, small amounts at a time. Shape the dough into a ball, put into a polythene bag or wrap in cling film and chill until firm.

Dust the work surface with a mixture of caster sugar and flour. Roll out the chilled dough until $\frac{1}{8}''$ (·25cm) thick. Cut out circles using a $2\frac{1}{2}''$ (6cm) fluted cutter and another circle inside those with a $1\frac{1}{2}''$ (3·5cm) cutter. Lift on to the baking tray with a palette knife and bake (just above the centre of the oven) in a preheated oven (375°F / Gas Mark 5 / 190°C) for 8–10 minutes or until lightly coloured around the edges. Dust with sifted icing sugar and cool on a wire rack. Pack in a tin or polythene bag (or container).

Makes about 3 dozen biscuits

CHOCOLATE BROWNIES

These can easily be made by the junior members of the picnic party – who will probably eat most of them anyway!

2oz (50g) butter, melted	2 large eggs
2oz (50g) cocoa powder	8oz (225g) sugar
4oz (100g) plain (flour	$\frac{1}{2}$ teaspoon vanilla
1 teaspoon baking powder	2oz–4oz (50g–100g) chopped
$\frac{1}{4}$ teaspoon salt	walnuts

Grease an 8″ (20cm) square tin (at least 1½″/3·5cm deep). Preheat oven to 350°F / Gas Mark 4 / 180°C.

Sift the flour, baking powder, cocoa powder and salt together on to a plate or sheet of greaseproof paper. Put the melted butter into a large mixing bowl and gradually mix in the sugar, the eggs, lightly beaten, and the vanilla. Sift the flour mixture over the top, and fold in with the chopped walnuts (stop folding the minute all the flour has been blended in). Pour into the prepared tin, spreading into the corners with a spatula. Bake in the centre of the oven for about 25 minutes. Take out and leave to cool in the tin, then cut into squares. Pack in a plastic container, polythene bag or foil.

Makes about 20 brownies

ICEBOX BISCUITS

4oz (100g) butter, at room
   temperature
8oz (225g) sugar
1 large egg
1 teaspoon vanilla
grated rind of 1 lemon

6oz (175g) plain flour
1½ teaspoons baking powder
¼ teaspoon salt
chopped walnuts or
   glacé cherries to decorate

Put the butter in a large mixing bowl and soften with a wooden spoon. Add the sugar and cream until light. Beat the egg and mix in with the grated lemon rind and vanilla. Sift the flour, baking powder and salt together, then sift gradually into the butter mixture, blending in well. Flour hands and press the dough into a cylinder shape about 1½″ (3·5cm) in diameter. Wrap tightly in greaseproof paper and chill for 12 hours (or in a freezer for 3–4 hours).

Preheat the oven to 400°F / Gas Mark 6 / 200°C. Slice the dough thinly and put on to a greased baking tray about 2″ (5cm) apart. Decorate each round with a piece of chopped walnut or glacé cherry. Bake just above the centre of the oven for 8–10 minutes or until lightly browned. Cool on a wire rack and pack in a tin or polythene bag.

Makes about 3 dozen biscuits

Recipes for the following can be found in other parts of the book: Pumpkin Pie (p. 267), Apple Pie (p. 208), French Apricot Flan (p. 181), Cherry Tartlets (p. 212), Jubilee Bonne Bouches (p. 212), Quick Chocolate Cake (p. 251), Blackberry Coffee Cake (p. 258), Oatmeal Cake (p. 229).

11
DRINKS

At the picnic:
Wrap the ice in a blanket and put it under the seat of
the waggon. Claret cup is sure to be wanted, to be mixed
on the spot by one of the men of the party. I have
noticed that when a man has made a claret cup which
is appreciated he feels thoroughly satisfied and at peace
with the world in general.

from *Girls' Own Paper*, 1880

If the above properties of a claret cup had been better adver-
tised, it might well be challenging Pimm's and Buck's Fizz on
the picnic fields today. As it is, we have become very un-
adventurous and the 'liquid refreshment' at a picnic these days
is rarely inspired. More's the pity as these cool punches can
transform the most ordinary picnic into quite an occasion.

If you should decide to find out for yourself what the special
'properties' of claret cup are, simply make it up beforehand
and pour into a chilled Thermos. Pack the soda separately and
add just before serving. To transport ice-cubes and keep the
bottles chilled, see the introductory section on Keeping Food
Cold.

LEMONADE

Lemon Syrup:

3 large lemons   8oz (225g) sugar
                   4oz (100ml) water

Grate the rind of 1 lemon and put in a saucepan with the sugar and water. Heat gently until the sugar has dissolved, then bring to the boil and boil for 5 minutes. Cool, then add the strained juice of three lemons. To make the lemonade, use 1 part lemon syrup to 2 parts soda or plain water. Serve with lots of ice.

MINT LEMONADE

4 large lemons   3 small (8½oz/240ml) bottles
a few sprigs of fresh mint   ginger ale
        6oz–8oz (175g–225g) sugar (or to taste)

Squeeze and strain the lemon juice, add the sugar and stir until dissolved. Put into a chilled Thermos with a few sprigs of fresh mint and several ice-cubes. Pack the ginger ale separately and add just before serving.

Serves 4

ICED TEA

For each serving use:

10oz (275ml) hot strong tea   2–3 lemon slices
caster sugar to taste   1 sprig of mint
          a few ice-cubes

196

Pour the hot tea into a jug and add sugar to taste. Stir until the sugar has dissolved. Then add a few ice-cubes, the lemon slices and a sprig of mint. Stir until the tea has become quite cold (add more ice if necessary) and check for sweetness. Pour into a chilled Thermos. Pack additional ice-cubes in a separate Thermos and add to the glasses just before pouring out.

ICED COFFEE

A delicious way of making quick iced coffee.

For each serving use:

1–3 tablespoons 'Camp' coffee or any bottled coffee/chicory syrup

10oz (275ml) cold milk
a few ice-cubes

Dissolve the 'Camp' coffee in the cold milk and make it as strong or weak as you like. Pour into a chilled Thermos with a few ice-cubes and put the stopper in securely. Shake well before pouring out.

BLACKCURRANT FIZZ

4 large oranges
6 tablespoons blackcurrant syrup

4 (8½oz/240ml) bottles ginger ale

Squeeze and strain the juice of two oranges. Cut the other two into thin slices. Mix the juice and blackcurrant syrup together, then pour into a Thermos. Add the orange slices and a few ice-cubes (or pack these separately). Keep the bottles of ginger ale as cool as possible and add to the syrup when ready to serve.

Serves 4

SUMMER FRUIT PUNCH

7oz (200ml) strong hot tea
3oz (75g) sugar (or to taste)
8oz (225ml) orange juice
3 tablespoons lemon
  concentrate (undiluted)

2½ tablespoons lime juice
1 (8½oz/240ml) bottle soda
  water
1 (8½oz/240ml) bottle ginger
  ale

Mix the hot tea and sugar together and stir until the sugar has dissolved. Mix in the fruit juices and chill for several hours. Pour into a cold Thermos and add the soda water and ginger ale just before serving. (If it's not possible to keep the soda and ginger ale chilled, then bring along a supply of ice-cubes in another Thermos.)

Serves 4

CRANBERRY/ORANGE COCKTAIL

1¼ pints (700ml) orange juice   6 tablespoons cranberry sauce

2–3 small bottles of tonic water

Put the orange juice and cranberry sauce into the blender and mix until smooth, light and frothy. Strain into a jug and chill thoroughly (chill the tonic water at the same time). Then pour into a Thermos and pack with the bottles of tonic water (keeping these cold if possible). When serving, mix the cranberry cocktail to taste with tonic water (1 part tonic to 2 parts cocktail is usually a good proportion). And while the children drink this, the adults can improve upon it by the addition of a small amount of gin, if they wish.

Makes about 2 pints (1·1 litres)

BUCK'S FIZZ

1 bottle of champagne or
sparkling white wine

1 litre carton of orange juice

Chill both the orange juice and sparkling wine well, then pack
in an insulated bag or next to the ice-packs in the picnic basket.
When ready to serve, mix 2 parts wine to 1 part orange juice, or
to taste. (Don't forget a pair of scissors to open the orange juice
carton with.)

Serves 4

EGG NOG

2 large eggs
2 egg yolks
2oz (50g) sugar
½ teaspoon vanilla

2oz (50ml) brandy
5oz (150ml) single cream
½ pint (275ml) rich milk
sprinkling of grated nutmeg

Beat the eggs, yolks, sugar and vanilla together until light.
Gradually beat in the brandy, cream and milk. Chill well, then
whisk again until frothy (or put in the blender) and pour into
a chilled Thermos. Shake the Thermos vigorously from side to
side before pouring out. Then sprinkle each glass with grated
nutmeg.

Serves 4

MILKSHAKES

For each milkshake use:
2 tablespoons tinned or fresh
fruit
½ dessertspoon sugar
(or to taste)

6oz (175ml) cold milk
1 large scoop of vanilla ice-
cream

Put all the ingredients into a blender and mix on high speed until light and frothy. Pour into a chilled Thermos. Shake vigorously before pouring out.

SANGRIA

1 large orange	1 bottle red wine (preferably
1 large lemon	Spanish), well chilled
2 dessert apples	2 small (8½oz/240ml) bottles
3–4 tablespoons sugar	soda water, chilled

3oz (75ml) brandy

Slice the oranges and lemons thinly. Wash and core the apples, then slice. Mix the brandy and sugar together and stir until the sugar has completely dissolved. Divide the brandy and fruit between two chilled Thermos flasks, then fill each one three-quarters full with red wine. Just before serving, top each Thermos up with cold soda water and stir well.

MOSELLE CUP*

juice and rind of 1 lemon	few thin slices of cucumber
5oz (150ml) Curaçao	1 (17oz/500ml) bottle soda
2 tablespoons sugar (or to	water
taste)	ice-cubes or crushed ice
1 bottle Moselle, well chilled	

Peel the rind very thinly off the lemon, then squeeze and strain all the juice. Mix with the Curaçao and sugar. Stir until the sugar has completely dissolved, then divide the mixture between two chilled Thermos flasks. Fill each one three-quarters full with the chilled white wine, add the cucumber slices and, if you like, ice-cubes or a small amount of crushed ice. Just before serving, top each Thermos up with soda water and stir well.

Serves 4

* Mrs Beeton's best

CLARET CUP

1 bottle of claret
5oz (150ml) sherry or brandy
2oz (50ml) Maraschino juice
peel of half a lemon

caster sugar to taste
crushed ice
1 (17oz/500ml) bottle soda water

Mix all the ingredients together, except the ice and soda water. Add sugar to taste. Stir until the sugar has dissolved, then pour into a chilled Thermos. Add a small amount of crushed ice, stir again and put the stopper in securely. Pack the soda water separately (keeping chilled if possible) and add to the wine just before serving.

Serves 6

SOMERSET CIDER PUNCH

8 tablespoons frozen orange-juice concentrate
4 tablespoons soft brown sugar
4oz (100ml) boiling water
6 cinnamon sticks
8 cloves
½ teaspoon ground mixed spice

4oz (100ml) undiluted lemon squash
2 large oranges
2 large (dessert) apples
a few ice-cubes
2–3 small (8½oz/240ml) bottles ginger ale

2 pints (1·1 litres) cider, chilled

Let the frozen orange juice thaw completely, then put into a large jug or bowl with the sugar and boiling water. Stir until the sugar has completely dissolved, then add the spices, cider and lemon squash. Wash and dry the fruit well, then slice thinly without peeling. Add to the drink and pour into two chilled Thermos flasks. Add several ice-cubes to each one, then put the stoppers in securely. Pack the ginger ale separately, and add to the punch just before serving.

Serves 6

HOT SPICED TEA

2 pints (1·1 litres) hot strong tea
2oz–4oz (50g–100g) sugar (to taste)

4oz (100ml) orange juice
1 lemon
6 cloves
4 cinnamon sticks

Put the tea and sugar into a large saucepan and stir until the sugar has dissolved. Squeeze and strain the juice from the lemon and add to the pan with the orange juice, cloves and cinnamon sticks. Heat slowly until steaming (taking care not to let it boil), then pour into a warmed Thermos.

Serves 6

HOT BRANDIED CIDER

2 pints (1·1 litres) cider
1 lemon
8 cloves

6 cinnamon sticks
4–6 tablespoons brandy
sugar to taste

Put all the ingredients except the sugar into a large saucepan and heat slowly until steaming (being careful not to let it boil). Add sugar to taste and stir until completely dissolved (if using a medium or sweet cider, no sugar may be necessary). Then pour into a warmed Thermos.

Serves 6

HOT RUM TODDY

For each serving use:
3½–4 tablespoons lemon
   concentrate (sweetened)

8oz (225ml) boiling water
3–4 tablespoons light rum

Mix the rum and lemon concentrate together, then add the boiling water. Stir until well blended and adjust (if necessary) to suit personal taste. Then pour into a warmed Thermos.

HOT CHOCOLATE WITH MARSHMALLOWS

2 pints (1·1 litres) milk
4 tablespoons cocoa powder

4 tablespoons sugar
   (or to taste)
white marshmallows

Put the milk, cocoa powder and sugar into a saucepan. Heat slowly until steaming. Add a handful of white marshmallows and pour at once into a warmed Thermos. (Or, if you prefer, pack the marshmallows separately and top each mug with one when the hot cocoa is poured out.)

Serves 6

GLUHWEIN

1 bottle red wine
2oz–3oz (50g–75g) sugar
4 cinnamon sticks

8 cloves
1 large lemon
2 large oranges

Put the wine in a large saucepan with the sugar, cinnamon sticks, and cloves. Pare the rind thinly of one orange and the lemon, then add to the pan. Squeeze and strain all the juice from the lemon and one orange and add with the remaining orange, sliced thinly. Heat slowly until steaming (don't let it boil), then stir well and pour into a warmed Thermos.

Serves 4

MULLED CIDER

3 small (11½oz/227ml) tins sweet cider
2 large (15½oz/540ml) tins dry cider
3 apples
2 oranges

1 lemon
4 cinnamon sticks
8 cloves
2 teaspoons ground mixed spice
6 tablespoons soft brown sugar

Wash and core the apples, then cut into medium slices. Wipe the skins well, then slice the oranges. Pare the rind off the lemon in thin strips, then squeeze and strain all the juice. Pour it into a large saucepan and add the apple and orange slices, spices, sugar and cider. Heat slowly until steaming, stir well, then pour into a warmed Thermos.

Serves 8

IRISH COFFEE

For each serving, use:
8oz (225ml) freshly made coffee

2 tablespoons Irish whiskey
1–2 tablespoons double cream
1 tablespoon sugar (or to taste)

Mix all the ingredients, except the cream, together and stir until the sugar has dissolved. Pour into a warmed Thermos. Pack the cream in its own container. When the coffee has been poured out, pour a small amount of double cream over the back of a spoon into each cup.

BORGIA COFFEE

2 pints (1·1 litres) freshly made
  strong coffee
pared rind and juice of large
  orange
2 tablespoons cocoa powder

10oz (275ml) milk
2 tablespoons sugar
  (or to taste)
1–2 tablespoons orange liqueur
  or brandy

Pare the rind thinly off the orange (avoiding the white pith).
Put it into a saucepan and pour over the freshly made coffee.
Leave to steep for 5 minutes. Add the milk, cocoa powder and
sugar. Stir until the sugar has dissolved, then heat until steaming
(be careful not to let it boil). Stir in the liqueur and pour into
a warmed Thermos.

Serves 6

Recipes for the following can be found in other parts of the book:
Pineapple Julep (p. 209), An Admirable Cool Cup (p. 215).

12

PICNICS IN FICTION

*Three Men in a Boat Picnic**

(*A Boating Picnic*)

To return to our present trip: nothing exciting happened, and we tugged steadily on to a little below Monkey Island, where we drew up and lunched. We tackled the cold beef for lunch, and then found we had forgotten to bring any mustard. I don't think I ever in my life, before or since, felt I wanted mustard as badly as I felt I wanted it then. I don't care for mustard as a rule, and it is very seldom that I take it at all, but I would have given worlds for it then.

Any picnicker, however seasoned, will appreciate the frustration felt by the 'three men in a boat' when the absence of the mustard becomes apparent. Sheer disbelief that this small oversight could have happened is soon replaced by acute dismay at its consequences. The object, which until that moment had seemed of little importance, suddenly assumes monumental proportions. The whole success of the picnic depends on it!

But as if this wasn't enough, minutes later, the tin-opener is discovered missing . . .

We are very fond of pineapple, all three of us. We looked at the picture on the tin; we thought of the juice. We smiled at one another, and Harris got a spoon ready.

* Taken from *Three Men in a Boat* by Jerome K. Jerome, 1889.

Then we looked for the knife to open the tin with. We turned out everything in the hamper. We turned out the bags. We pulled up the boards at the bottom of the boat. We took everything out on to the bank and shook it. There was no tin-opener to be found.

Recipes for the picnic are taken from *Mrs Beeton's Book of Household Management*, 1881 and early twentieth-century editions.

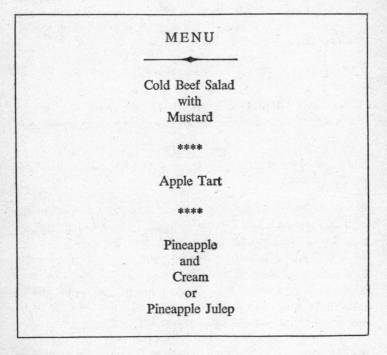

MENU

◆

Cold Beef Salad
with
Mustard

****

Apple Tart

****

Pineapple
and
Cream
or
Pineapple Julep

COLD MEAT SALAD

(For those who don't trust themselves to remember the mustard and would prefer to put it in first.)

Ingredients: 1½lb of cold roast or boiled meat, 4 anchovy fillets, 2 shallots, 2 tablespoonfuls of salad-oil, 1 tablespoonful of wine vinegar, ½ a teaspoonful of finely-chopped parsley, 1 teaspoonful of French mustard, salt and pepper. For garnishing: Finely-shredded pickled gherkins, finely-chopped capers.

Method: Cut the meat into strips about 2½ inches in length and 1 inch in width. Chop the shallots and fillets of anchovy finely, put them into a basin, add ½ a teaspoonful of parsley, the oil, vinegar and mustard, season with a little salt and pepper, then stir in the slices of meat, cover, and put aside for 2 hours, stirring occasionally. When ready to serve, arrange the salad in a pyramidal form in a salad-bowl, garnish with strips of gherkin and chopped capers, and serve.

Time: About 2½ hours   *Sufficient* for 6 or 7 persons

APPLE TART OR PIE

Ingredients: Puff-pastry, apples; to every lb of unpared apples allow 2oz of moist sugar, ½ teaspoonful of finely minced lemon-peel, 1 tablespoonful of lemon-juice.

Mode: Make ½lb of puff-paste, place a border of it round the edge of a pie-dish, and fill it with apples, pared, cored, and cut into slices; sweeten with moist sugar, add the lemon-peel and juice, and 2 or 3 tablespoonfuls of water; cover with crust, cut it evenly round close to the edge of the pie-dish, and bake in a hot oven from ½ to ¾ hour, or rather longer, should the pie be very large. When it is three-parts done, take it out of the oven, put the white of an egg on a plate, and, with the blade of a knife, whisk it to a froth; brush the pie over with this, then sprinkle upon it some sifted sugar, and then a few drops of water. Put the pie back into the oven, and finish baking, and be particularly careful that it does not catch or burn, which it is very liable to do after the crust is iced. If made with a plain crust, the icing may be omitted.

Time: ½ hour before the crust is iced; 10–15 minutes afterwards
Average cost: 9d

PINEAPPLE JULEP

A reward for those who remember the tin-opener . . .

Ingredients: 1 pineapple either fresh or preserved, 1 bottle of sparkling Moselle, 1 gill* of gin, 1 gill of raspberry syrup, $\frac{1}{2}$ a gill of Maraschino, the juice of 2 oranges, 1lb of crushed ice.

Method: Slice the pineapple rather thinly, and divide each slice into 8 sections. Put all the liquids into a glass jug or bowl, add the ice and prepared pineapple, and serve.

* 5oz (150ml).

The Go-Between Picnic*

(*A Summer Picnic*)

'The past is a foreign country; they do things differently there.'

The summer of 1900 is well recorded in the diary of Leo, namesake and narrator of *The Go-Between*. From the moment he arrives at Brandham Hall, he becomes conscious of the special role he is to play. As the fleet-footed Mercury, he provides the life-line between Marion and Ted. The weight of this conspiracy and the novelty of his situation make him unusually aware of what is going on around him:

> One remembers things at different levels. I still have an impression, distinct but hard to analyse, of the change that came over the household with Lord Trimingham's arrival.
> Picnics or expeditions or visits were planned for almost every day: Mrs Maudsley would announce them after breakfast . . .

* Taken from *The Go-Between* by L. P. Hartley, 1953.

. . . I can remember sitting by some stream and watching the hampers being unpacked, the rugs spread out, and the footmen bending down to change our plates. The grown-ups drank amber wine out of tall tapering bottles; I was given fizzy lemonade from a bottle with a glass marble for a stopper. I enjoyed the meal; it was the conversation afterwards, while the things were being packed away, that was the strain.

Unfortunately for us, Leo becomes so preoccupied with the conversation at the picnic that he tells us very little about the food. We can only imagine that, in spite of temperatures in the 80's, it would be true to Victorian standards with generous quantities of both food and drink.

Recipes for the picnic are taken from the 'July' section of the *Day by Day Cookery Book*, published in 1900, the same year that Leo's diary was written.

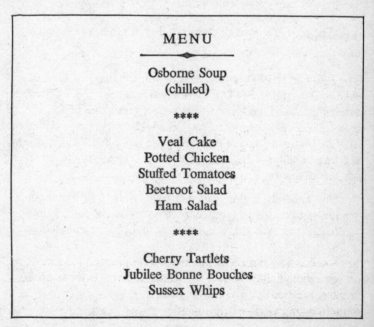

MENU

◆

Osborne Soup
(chilled)

****

Veal Cake
Potted Chicken
Stuffed Tomatoes
Beetroot Salad
Ham Salad

****

Cherry Tartlets
Jubilee Bonne Bouches
Sussex Whips

OSBORNE SOUP

Put 1 quart of peas into 3 pints of boiling stock, with 1 teaspoonful of salt, a sprig of mint, 3 sliced onions, a little pepper, and 1 lump of sugar; boil until soft, and then rub through a taminy,* and serve with a little finely minced mint added at the moment of serving. If the colour is not very good, a few drops of Marshall's spinach juice will greatly improve it.

* a fine mesh strainer

VEAL CAKE

Rinse out a small cake mould with cold water, then decorate the bottom with slices of hard-boiled egg, sprinkle a little parsley and grated lemon peel over; now cut up 1lb of lean veal into small pieces, also ½lb fat bacon, fill the mould with this, add pepper and salt to taste and more egg on top, pour in ¼ pint of strong white stock; cover the top over with a piece of greased paper, and bake in a slow oven for four hours; when quite cold turn out, garnish with capsicums and parsley.

POTTED CHICKEN

Take all the meat from the bones of the cold chicken; put it through a sausage machine, and then pound it in a mortar with ¼ pound of butter, a little cayenne, and 3 anchovies; when quite smooth fill a fancy pot, press down, and cover with liquid butter.

STUFFED TOMATOES

Cut some large tomatoes into halves, scoop out some of the pulp, and fill with highly seasoned sausage meat, cover with bread crumbs, put some small pieces of butter on top and bake in a moderate oven for twenty minutes.

BEETROOT SALAD

Peel the beetroot and cut it in slices with a fancy cutter, and lay on a dish 3 slices of beet and 3 of cold boiled potato alternately until the dish is full; make a dressing of oil, vinegar, and salt and pepper, and pour over the salad; now sprinkle a few capers and a small quantity of finely chopped parsley on top.

HAM SALAD

Pull 1 lettuce into small pieces, and put it in a bowl with a few slices of cucumber, beetroot, a soupçon of onion, a little finely minced ham, 2 anchovies, and a few olives; sprinkle over 1 teaspoonful of chopped sorrel; cover with mayonnaise sauce; garnish with cut gherkins, the hard-boiled yolk of 1 egg which has been rubbed through a wire sieve, and small slices of rolled ham.

CHERRY TARTLETS

Boil ¾ pint of milk with 3oz of caster sugar and 1 strip of lemon peel; strain, add 1½oz of ground rice, and boil slowly for ten minutes; then turn into a basin, add 2 beaten eggs, 1 oz of butter, and 6 chopped cherries; line some patty-pans with paste, fill with the custard, and bake for 20 minutes in a fairly hot oven.

JUBILEE BONNE BOUCHES

Line some small patty-pans with rich pastry, and half-fill with the following mixture, and bake in a moderate oven for about ten minutes: Beat 2oz of butter until perfectly smooth, then add 2oz of caster sugar, and beat well; mix in 2 yolks of eggs and beat again, then 1 tablespoonful of cream, put in a few currants and finely chopped citron; beat all the ingredients well together before putting in the patty-pans.

SUSSEX WHIPS

Mix well together in a basin $\frac{1}{2}$ pint of thick cream, $\frac{1}{2}$ pint of brandy, $\frac{1}{4}$lb of powdered sugar, a squeeze of lemon juice, and 1 lump of sugar that has been rubbed on a rind of a lemon; when mixed thoroughly whisk the whole in a large basin, and as the froth rises take it off with a spoon, and fill custard cups.

*A Pickwick Picnic**

(*A Shooting Picnic*)

Anyone who has been carried away by the excitement of a picnic to the extent of over-indulging will sympathize with Mr Pickwick's predicament after the shooting picnic on One-Tree Hill. His enthusiasm for the cold punch on that occasion was such that he fell sound asleep in the wheelbarrow (his mode of transport for the day, being laid up with rheumatism). And during this time he was literally carried away to the pound by the servant of an irate landowner. He awoke to find himself the laughing-stock of the town!

But the picnic, reading from Dickens's description, sounds well worth it:

'Weal pie,' said Mr Weller, soliloquising, as he arranged the eatables on the grass. 'Wery good thing is weal pie, when you know the lady as made it, and is quite sure it an't kittens; and arter all though, where's the odds, when they're so like weal that the very piemen themselves don't know the difference?'

. . . 'Just was, sir,' replied Mr Weller, continuing his occupation of emptying the basket, 'and the pies was beautiful. Tongue; well that's a wery good thing when it

* Taken from *The Pickwick Papers* by Charles Dickens, 1836–7.

an't a woman's. Bread – knuckle o' ham, reg'lar picter – cold beef in slices, wery good. What's in them stone jars, young touch-and-go?'

'Beer in this one,' replied the boy, taking from his shoulder a couple of large stone bottles, fastened together by a leathern strap – 'cold punch in t'other.'

'And a wery good notion of a lunch it is, take it altogether,' said Mr Weller, surveying his arrangement of the repast with great satisfaction. 'Now, gen'l'm'n, "fall on," as the English said to the French when they fixed bagginets.'

Recipes for the picnic are taken from *Modern Cookery for Private Families* by Eliza Acton, first published in 1845, and from *The Modern Cook* by Francatelli, published in 1846.

MENU

———◆———

Veal Pie

Cold Tongue

Cold Beef

Cold Ham

Bread and Cheese

Beer

Cold Punch

VEAL AND HAM PIE

Trim the veal and ham into scallops, and season with pepper and salt in moderation. Next chop a handful of mushrooms and some parsley very fine, and put them in a small stewpan with a small pat of butter, and one shalot also chopped fine; fry these lightly over the fire, then add nearly a pint of Velouté sauce or good stock; boil the whole for five minutes, and pour it into the pie; place six yolks of eggs boiled hard in the cavities, cover with puff-paste, bake the pie for an hour and a half, and serve.

From Francatelli's *The Modern Cook*

AN ADMIRABLE COOL CUP

Weigh six ounces of sugar in lumps, and extract the essence from the rind of a large fresh lemon by rubbing them upon it; then put them into a deep jug, and add the strained juice of one lemon and a half. When the sugar is dissolved, pour in a bottle of good cider, and three large wineglassesful of sherry; add nearly half a small nutmeg lightly grated, and serve the cup with or without some sprigs of fresh balm or borage in it. Brandy is sometimes added to it, but is, we think, no improvement. If closely covered down and placed on ice for a short time, it will be more agreeable as a summer beverage.

From Eliza Acton's *Modern Cookery for Private Families*

*A Wind in the Willows Picnic**

(*A Riverbank Picnic*)

In which Rat introduces his new-found friend, Mole, to the delights of the River . . .

'Hold hard a minute, then!' said the Rat. He looped the painter through a ring in his land-stage, climbed up into his hole above, and after a short interval reappeared staggering under a fat, wicker luncheon basket.

'Shove that under your feet,' he observed to the Mole, as he passed it down into the boat. Then he untied the painter and took the sculls again.

'What's inside it?' asked the Mole, wriggling with curiosity.

'There's cold chicken inside it,' replied the Rat briefly; coldtonguecoldhamcoldbeefpickledgherkinssaladfrench rollscresssandwidgespottedmeatgingerbeerlemonadesoda water – '

'O stop, stop,' cried the Mole in ecstasies: 'This is too much!'

'Do you really think so?' inquired the Rat seriously. 'It's only what I always take on these little excursions; and the other animals are always telling me that I'm a mean beast and cut it *very* fine!'

Recipes for the picnic are taken from *Mrs Beeton's Every Day Cookery*, 1907 edition.

* Taken from *The Wind in the Willows* by Kenneth Grahame, 1908.

MENU

◆

Cold Tongue

Cold Beef

Cold Ham

Pickled Gherkins

Salad

French Rolls

Cress Sandwiches

Potted Meat

Ginger Beer

Lemonade/Soda Water

The Rat brought that boat alongside the bank, made her fast, helped the still awkward Mole safely ashore, and swung out the luncheon-basket. The Mole begged as a favour to be allowed to unpack it all by himself; and the Rat was very pleased to indulge him, and to sprawl at full length on the grass and rest, while his excited friend shook out the table-cloth and spread it, took out all the contents in due order, still gasping, 'O my! O my!' at each fresh revelation. When all was ready, the Rat said, 'Now pitch in, old fellow!' and the Mole was indeed very glad to obey, for he had started his spring-cleaning at a very early hour that morning, as people *will* do, and had not paused for bite or sup; and he had been through a very great deal since that distant time which now seemed so many days ago.

GHERKINS, Pickled

Ingredients: Salt and water, 1oz of bruised ginger, ½oz of whole black pepper, ¼oz of whole black spice, 4 cloves, 2 blades of mace, a little horseradish. This proportion of pepper, spices, etc., for 1 quart of vinegar.

Let the gherkins remain in salt and water for 3 or 4 days, when take them out, wipe perfectly dry, and put them into a stone jar. Boil sufficient vinegar to cover them, with spices and pepper, etc., in the above proportion, for 10 minutes; pour it, quite boiling, over the gherkins, cover the jar with vine-leaves, and put over them a plate, setting them near the fire, where they must remain all night. Next day drain off the vinegar, boil it up again, and pour it hot over them. Cover up with fresh leaves and let the whole remain till quite cold. Now tie closely with bladder to exclude the air, and in a month or two they will be fit for use.

Time: 4 days
Seasonable from the middle of July to the end of August

SALAD, Summer

Ingredients: for salad for 8 persons – 3 lettuces, 2 handfuls of mustard-and-cress, 10 young radishes, a few slices of cucumber.
Average cost: with dressing, 10d

Let the herbs be as fresh as possible for a salad, and, if at all stale or dead-looking, let them lie in water for an hour or two, which will very much refresh them. Wash and carefully pick them over, remove decayed or worm-eaten leaves, and drain them thoroughly by swinging them gently in a clean cloth. With a silver knife, cut the lettuces into small pieces, and the radishes and cucumbers into thin slices; arrange all these ingredients lightly on a dish, with the mustard-and-cress, and pour under, but not over, the salad either of the salad-dressings, and do not stir it up until it is to be eaten.

FRENCH ROLLS

Ingredients: Puff-paste, the white of an egg, sifted sugar, jelly or preserve.

Make some good puff-paste (trimmings answer very well for little dishes of this sort); roll it out to the thickness of ¼ inch, and with a round fluted paste-cutter stamp out as many round pieces as may be required; brush over the upper side with the white of an egg; roll up the pieces, pressing the paste lightly together where it joins; place the rolls on a baking-sheet, and bake for about ¼ hour. A few minutes before they are done, brush them over with the white of an egg, strew over sifted sugar, put them back in the oven, and when the icing is firm and of a pale brown colour, they are done. Place a strip of jelly or preserve across each roll, dish them high on a napkin, and serve cold.

Time: ¼ hour before being iced; 5 to 10 minutes after
Seasonable at any time

BEEF, Potted

Ingredients: The remains of cold roast or boiled beef, butter, cayenne to taste, blades of pounded mace.

The outside slices of boiled beef may, with a little trouble, be converted into a very nice addition to the breakfast table. Cut up the meat into small pieces and pound it well with a little butter, in a mortar; add a seasoning of cayenne and mace, and be very particular that the latter spice is reduced to the finest powder. When all the ingredients are thoroughly mixed, put them into glass or earthenware potting-pots, and pour on the top a coating of clarified butter.

Seasonable at any time

Mr Cheesacre's Picnic*

(*A Marine Picnic*)

. . . it was to be a marine picnic, and therefore the essential attributes of other picnics were not required. The idea had come from some boating expeditions, in which mackerel had been caught, and during which foods had been eaten, not altogether comfortably, in the boats. Then a thought had suggested itself to Captain Bellfield that they might land and eat their food, and his friend Mr Cheesacre had promised his substantial aid. A lady had surmised that Ormesby sands would be the very place for dancing in the cool of the evening. They might 'Dance on the sand,' she said, 'and yet no footing seen.' And so the thing had progressed, and the picnic been inaugurated.

Trollope describes with some amusement the combined efforts needed to produce a picnic on the sands. Mr Cheesacre's fears that he might be left to organize the entire picnic on his own are quickly allayed by Mrs Greenow who agrees to bring the meat, pastry and fruit. But at the same time, Cheesacre wants to make quite sure everyone knows whose picnic it is and see to it that his 'substantial aid' does not go unnoticed . . .

It was Mr Cheesacre's picnic undoubtedly. Mr Cheesacre was to supply the boats, the wine, the cigars, the music

* Taken from *Can You Forgive Her?* by Anthony Trollope, 1864–5.

and the carpenter's work necessary for the turning of the old boat into a banqueting saloon. But Mrs Greenow had promised to provide the eatables . . .

. . . there was a long, dry, flat strand; there was an old boat half turned over, under which it was proposed to dine; and in addition to this, benches, boards, and some amount of canvas for shelter were provided by the liberality of Mr Cheesacre. Therefore it was called Mr Cheesacre's picnic.

Recipes for the picnic are taken from *Mrs Beeton's Book of Household Management*, published in 1861.

MENU

◆

Cold Ham
Cold Chicken
Grouse Pie

***

Boiled Salad
Cucumber Salad
Salad Dressing

***

Apricot Pie

***

Cheese and Fruit

***

Wine

GROUSE PIE

Ingredients:

1 grouse
cayenne
salt and pepper to taste

1lb rump steak
½ pint of well-seasoned broth
puff paste

Mode:

Line the bottom of a pie-dish with the rump-steak cut into neat pieces, and, should the grouse be large, cut them into joints; but, if small, they may be laid in the pie whole; season highly with salt, cayenne, and black pepper; pour in the broth, and cover with a puff paste; brush the crust over with the yolk of an egg, and bake from ¾ to 1 hour. If the grouse is cut into joints, the backbones and trimmings will make the gravy, by stewing them with an onion, a little sherry, a bunch of herbs, and a blade of mace: this should be poured in after the pie is baked.

Time: ¾ to 1 hour

Average cost: exclusive of the grouse, which are seldom bought, 1s 9d

Seasonable from the 12th of August to the beginning of December

BOILED SALAD

Ingredients:

2 heads of celery
1 pint of French beans

lettuce
endive

Mode:

Boil the celery and beans separately until tender, and cut the celery into pieces about 2 inches long. Put these into a salad-bowl or dish; pour over either of the sauces No. 518, 519 or 520 and garnish the dish with a little lettuce finely chopped, blanched endive, or a few tufts of boiled cauliflower. This composition, if less agreeable than vegetables in their raw state, is more wholesome; for salads, however they may be compounded, when eaten uncooked, prove to some people indigestible. Tarragon, chervil, burnet, and boiled onion, may be added to the above salad with advantage, as also slices of cold meat, poultry or fish.

Seasonable from July to October

SALAD DRESSING 518

Ingredients:

1 teaspoon mixed mustard
1 teaspoon pounded sugar
2 tablespoons salad oil

4 tablespoons milk
2 tablespoons vinegar
cayenne and salt to taste

Mode:
Put the mixed mustard into a salad-bowl with the sugar, and add the oil drop by drop, carefully stirring and mixing all these ingredients well together. Proceed in this manner with the milk and vinegar, which must be added very *gradually*, or the sauce will curdle. Put in the seasoning, when the mixture will be ready for use. If this dressing is properly made, it will have a soft and creamy appearance, and will be found very delicious with crab, or cold fried fish (the latter cut into dice), as well as with salads. In mixing salad dressings, the ingredients cannot be added *too gradually*, or *stirred too much*.

Average cost: for this quantity, 3*d*
Sufficient for a small salad

SALAD DRESSING 519

Ingredients:

4 eggs
1 teaspoon mixed mustard
¼ teaspoon white pepper

half that quantity of cayenne
4 tablespoons cream
salt to taste
vinegar

Mode:

Boil the eggs until hard, which will be in about ¼ hour or 20 minutes; put them into cold water, take off the shells, and pound the yolks in a mortar to a smooth paste. Then add all the other ingredients, except the vinegar, and stir them well until the whole are thoroughly incorporated one with the other. Pour in sufficient vinegar to make it of the consistency of cream, taking care to add but little at a time. The mixture will then be ready for use.

Average cost: for this quantity, 7*d*
Sufficient for a moderate-sized salad
Note: The whites of the eggs, cut into rings, will serve very well as a garnishing to the salad.

CUCUMBER SALAD

Ingredients:

1 large or 2 small cucumbers
½ teaspoon pepper and salt mixed
1 tablespoon best French vinegar
3 tablespoons pure salad oil

Mode:

Peel and slice the cucumber as finely as possible, sprinkle the pepper and salt over it; add vinegar and oil in the above proportions a moment before using.

Time: 5 minutes
Average cost: 6*d* to 9*d* in full season
Sufficient for 5 persons
Seasonable in May, June and July

APRICOT PIE

Ingredients:

12 or 14 apricots   puff-paste or short crust
sugar to taste

Mode:

Break the apricots in half, take out the stones, and put them into a pie-dish, in the centre of which place a very small cup or jar, bottom uppermost; sweeten with good moist sugar, but add no water. Line the edge of the dish with paste, put on the cover, and ornament the pie in any of the usual modes. Bake from ½ to ¾ hour, according to size; and if puff-paste is used, glaze it about 10 minutes before the pie is done, and put it into the oven again to set the glaze. Short crust merely requires a little sifted sugar sprinkled over it before being sent to the table.

Time: ½ to ¾ hour
Average cost: in full season, 1s
Sufficient for 4 or 5 persons
Seasonable in August, September and October; green ones rather earlier

The Secret Garden Picnic*

(*A Picnic Tea*)

They saw the robin carry food to his mate two or three times, and it was so suggestive of afternoon tea that Colin felt they must have some.

* Taken from *The Secret Garden* by Frances Hodgson Burnett, 1911.

'Go and make one of the menservants bring some in a basket to the rhododendron walk,' he said. 'And then you and Dickon can bring it here.'

It was an agreeable idea; easily carried out, and when the white cloth was spread upon the grass, with hot tea and buttered toast and crumpets, a delightfully hungry meal was eaten . . . Nut and Shell whisked up trees with pieces of cake, and Soot took the entire half of a buttered crumpet . . .

Eating outdoors always increases the appetite, but when eating outdoors, *and* in secret, it knows no bounds. Colin, Dickon and Mary soon discovered this when they had their first taste of toast and crumpets in the garden. The Yorkshire air may have been partly responsible but, according to Colin, it was all due to the 'Magic' of the place. Dickon's mother, Mrs Sowerby, was found to have equally magic qualities when she sent a surprise picnic (the first of many) to the garden . . .

The morning that Dickon – after they had been enjoying themselves in the garden for about two hours – went behind a big rose-bush and brought forth two tin pails and revealed that one was full of rich new milk with cream on the top of it, and that the other held cottage-made currant buns folded in a clean blue and white napkin, buns so carefully tucked in that they were still hot. There was a riot of surprised joyfulness. What a kind, clever woman she must be! How good the buns were! And what delicious fresh milk!

Recipes for the picnic are taken from old Yorkshire cookbooks.

MENU

◆

Currant Buns

Buttered Toast

Crumpets

***

Cake

***

Hot Tea

Cold Milk

CURRANT BUNS

10oz (275g) plain flour
2 teaspoons baking powder
4oz (100g) butter
4oz (100g) caster sugar
1½oz (40g) chopped candied peel

4oz (100g) currants
2 large eggs
1–2 tablespoons milk
milk to glaze
caster sugar

Grease a large baking tray.
Preheat oven to 400°F / Gas Mark 6 / 200°C.

Sift the flour and baking powder together into a large mixing bowl. Rub in the butter until the mixture resembles bread-crumbs. Add the sugar, candied peel and currants and mix in well. Beat the eggs lightly and add with just enough milk to make a soft, scone-like dough.

Turn out on to a lightly floured counter and roll out to a $\frac{1}{2}$" (1cm) thickness. Cut into 2" (5cm) squares and fold over to make triangles. Brush lightly with milk and sprinkle with caster sugar. Place well apart on the baking tray and bake in the centre of the oven for 15 minutes or until lightly browned. Take out and cool on a wire rack. Store and pack in a polythene bag or container. Serve on their own or split open and buttered.

Makes about 18 currant buns

YORKSHIRE SPICE BREAD*
(for Buttered Toast)

12oz (350g) plain flour
2 teaspoons baking powder
$\frac{1}{2}$ teaspoon bicarbonate of soda
3oz (75g) butter
6oz (175g) demerara sugar

3oz (75g) currants
3oz (75g) sultanas
1$\frac{1}{2}$oz (40g) chopped candied
   peel
2 large eggs

6oz (175ml) milk

Grease a 2lb (9"/23cm) loaf tin.
Preheat oven to 325°F / Gas Mark 3 / 170°C.

Sift the flour, baking powder and bicarbonate of soda together into a mixing bowl and rub in the butter. Add the sugar, currants, sultanas, chopped peel and mix in well. Make a well in the centre and pour in the eggs, lightly beaten, and the milk. Gradually draw in the flour from around the sides and mix until completely blended. Pour into prepared tin and bake in the centre of the oven for 1–1$\frac{1}{4}$ hours or until a toothpick inserted

---

* This is not a misnomer; there are several different recipes for this bread but none of them includes spice!

in the centre comes out clean. Reverse out on to a wire rack, stand right side up and leave to cool. Store and pack in a polythene bag. Serve plain or toasted with butter.

Makes 1 large loaf

OATMEAL CAKE

3oz (75ml) treacle
2oz (50ml) golden syrup
5oz (150ml) milk
12oz (350g) plain flour
1 teaspoon baking powder

1 teaspoon ground ginger
4oz (100g) butter
4oz (100g) soft brown sugar
4oz (100g) fine oatmeal
$\frac{1}{2}$ teaspoon bicarbonate of soda

Grease an 8" (20cm) square tin and line with greaseproof paper. Preheat oven to 325°F / Gas Mark 3 / 170°C.

Put the treacle, golden syrup and milk into a small saucepan and heat gently until completely blended. Take off the heat and cool to lukewarm.

Sift the flour, baking powder and ground ginger into a large bowl. Rub in the butter, then mix in the sugar and oatmeal. Dissolve the bicarbonate of soda in the cooled syrup. Make a well in the dry ingredients, tip in the syrup mixture and gradually draw in the flour from around the sides. When well blended, pour into prepared tin and level off with the back of a spoon. Bake in the centre of the oven for an hour or until a toothpick inserted in the centre comes out clean. Reverse out on a wire rack, stand right side up and leave to cool. Store and pack in a polythene bag or cling film. Serve sliced with butter.

Makes 1 large cake

13

INTERNATIONAL PICNICS

Italian Picnics

Madame, I have only cried twice in my life; once when
I dropped a wing of truffled chicken into Lake Como,
and once, when for the first time I heard you sing.

Rossini (congratulating Patti on her incomparable singing)

Eating al fresco is so much a part of the Italian way of life that
picnicking as such is almost superfluous. Why suffer in a field
full of ants or mosquitoes when you can eat in the comfort of
a vine-covered trattoria? But when the temperature rises, the
Italians head for the hills or the coast and here the picnics
flourish. With many offices closing after lunch during the
summer, by three o'clock they can be sitting comfortably on a
sunny beach. And at their feet, a picnic of mortadella, salami,
cheese, figs and wine, all purchased on the way.

SPRING PICNIC

Pizzette
(Miniature Pizzas)

***

Triglia alla Griglia
(Grilled Red Mullet)

Zucchine ripiene
(Stuffed courgettes)

***

Gorgonzola

Pesche e Ciliegie
(Fresh Peaches and Cherries)

***

Wine: Soave

SUMMER PICNIC

Prosciutto con melone
(Parma Ham and melon)

***

Insalata di gamberi
(Prawn Salad)

Pomodori con Fagiolini
(Tomatoes stuffed with haricot beans)

***

Gelato
(Ice-cream)

***

Wine: Verdicchio or Trebbiano

AUTUMN PICNIC

Salami

***

Pizza Napoletana

Insalata verde
(Green Salad)

Insalata di funghi
(Mushroom Salad)

***

Fichi e Uva
(Figs and Grapes)

***

Wine: Valpolicella

WINTER PICNIC

Minestrone

***

Manzo freddo a fette
(Cold sliced beef)

Insalata di Pasta alla melanzane
(Pasta Salad with aubergines)

***

Arancie Caramellizzate
(Caramel Oranges)

***

Wine: Chianti

Consult the index for recipes for the above.

ARANCIE CARAMELLIZZATE
(Caramel Oranges)

6 large oranges   6oz (175g) caster sugar
                    6oz (175ml) water

Peel the oranges, then slice thinly lengthwise. Put in a bowl and to one side.

Put the caster sugar with 4oz (100ml) of water into a heavy saucepan. Dissolve the sugar over gentle heat, without stirring (shake the pan occasionally), then bring to the boil. Boil rapidly until the sugar caramelizes and turns a rich golden brown. Add the remaining water and stir until completely blended. Carefully add the oranges and their juice, mix well in the syrup, then transfer to a bowl or plastic container. Chill for several hours then cover with a lid or cling film and pack.

Serves 4

INSALATA DI FUNGHI
(Mushroom Salad)

1lb (450g) fresh button mushrooms

Dressing:
2 tablespoons lemon juice   freshly chopped herbs
4 tablespoons olive oil   salt and pepper

Wash and drain the mushrooms well, then dry with absorbent kitchen paper. Slice thinly, then put in a bowl or plastic container. Mix all the dressing ingredients in a small jar until well blended. Pour over the mushrooms and toss carefully, using two spoons. Cover with a lid, foil or cling film and pack. This salad should be made the day of the picnic and, if possible, at the last minute.

Serves 4

French Picnics

A Provençal Picnic

Ford Madox Ford has described a Provençal picnic of heroic proportions; the scene was one of the beautiful calanques along the coast from Marseilles, a beach accessible only in boats; the whole banquet was cooked on the spot, in huge cauldrons, beneath the umbrella pines. Sixty-one bottles of wine were consumed by sixteen adults and a shoal of children; half a hundredweight of bouillabaisse, twelve cocks stewed in wine with innumerable savoury herbs, a salad in a dish as large as a cartwheel, sweet cream cheese with a sauce made of marc and sweet herbs, a pile, large enough to bury a man in, of apples, peaches, figs, grapes . . .

Elizabeth David in *Summer Cooking*

If only we could transplant the French boulangerie, patisserie and charcuterie to English soil! Then we would have, within a minute's walk, all the ingredients necessary for instant picnics at their best: fresh baguettes, still warm from the oven; pâté maison; jambon du pays and tarte aux fraises. Never again would we have to resort to pork pies and leaden fruit-cake in a desperate last-minute attempt to fill the picnic basket.

A BRITTANY PICNIC

Potage Cressonière
(Watercress Soup)

***

Crêpes bretonnes

Salade de saison

***

Groseilles
(Fresh Redcurrants)

au

Fromage blanc
(Soft white cheese)

***

Muscadet

NORMANDY PICNIC

Terrine de canard
(Terrine of duck)

***

Poulet Normand
(Chicken with Apples and Cider)

Choufleur polonais

Salade verte

***

Pêches
(Fresh Peaches)

Fromage: Pont L'Evêque
or
Camembert

***

Chablis

BOIS DE BOLOGNE PICNIC

◆

Pâté Maison

Baguette et la beurre sans du sel
(French bread and unsalted butter)

***

Saucisson
(Spicy sausage)

Jambon du pays
(Thinly sliced ham)

Salade de tomates
(Tomato Salad)

***

Tarte aux Abricots
(Apricot Flan)

***

Beaujolais

PROVENCAL PICNIC

Salade Niçoise

***

Pissaladière

Salade de haricots verts
(Green Bean Salad)

***

Crème Brûlée

***

Vin Rosé de Provence

Consult the index for recipes for the above.

GROSEILLES AU FROMAGE BLANC

1lb (450g) fresh redcurrants
sugar to taste

8oz (225g) fromage blanc (or
'fromage frais')*

Medium bowl or plastic container

Wash and drain the redcurrants well. Top and tail them, then put into a bowl and sprinkle with 1–2 tablespoons of sugar. Leave until the sugar has dissolved. Check for sweetness and add more sugar if necessary. Then spoon into a bowl or plastic container.

Tip the 'fromage blanc' into a bowl and whisk lightly until completely smooth. Add a small amount of sugar (but not too much as its slight tartness should complement the sweetened redcurrants) and whisk until well blended. Then pour over the redcurrants. Cover with a lid or cling film and chill until needed. When packing, try to put it at the bottom of the basket or near the ice-packs to keep it chilled (though this isn't absolutely necessary). Try also to keep it level.

Take along a large spoon and, just before serving, partly fold the 'fromage blanc' into the redcurrants. Dish into clear glasses or bowls so that the colourful contrast of red, white and pink is not missed.

Serves 4

* This is a soft, low-fat white cheese which has a runny consistency. It is packaged like yogurt and can be found in the cheese sections of large supermarkets or in the food halls of most department stores.

CREME BRULEE

2oz (50g) caster sugar
4 large egg yolks
¼ teaspoon vanilla essence
½ pint (275ml) single cream

½ pint (275ml) double cream

6oz (175g) caster sugar
6 tablespoons water

6 ramekin dishes
Preheat oven to 325°F / Gas Mark 3 / 170°C.

Put the egg yolks, sugar and vanilla essence into a bowl and stir with a fork or wooden spoon until well mixed. Blend in the cream, then strain the mixture into a jug. Pour into the ramekin dishes and stand these in a small roasting tin filled with an inch (2·5cm) of warm water. Place in the centre of the oven and bake for 45 minutes or until the custard has set. Take out and chill for several hours or overnight.

Put the sugar and water into a heavy saucepan and heat gently until the sugar has dissolved. Then boil rapidly until the syrup turns a rich caramel colour. Take off the heat at once and pour a small amount over each custard to seal. Refrigerate until set. Then cover with cling film and pack.

Serves 6

CREPES BRETONNES

Either use the recipe given earlier in the book for wholewheat crêpes or the version below which uses plain flour.

4oz (100g) plain flour
good pinch of salt
2 eggs, lightly beaten
½ pint (275ml) milk

1 tablespoon melted butter
butter or oil for cooking
melted butter to glaze

Sift the flour and salt into a mixing bowl. Make a well in the centre and pour in the beaten eggs. Draw in the flour gradually from around the sides and mix to a smooth paste. Then blend in the milk and, finally, the melted butter. Pour into a jug and let stand in a cool place for at least half an hour.

Cover the base of a heavy frying pan with oil or melted butter, then pour out any surplus. Heat until it begins to steam and pour in a small amount of batter, swirling the pan so that it is evenly distributed. Cook over moderate heat until the underside is golden brown, then flip over and cook the other side. Lift out with a palette knife and stack up on a plate (if leaving to cool, put a piece of greaseproof paper between each crêpe).

Put a dollop of filling in the centre of each crêpe, roll up and tuck the ends under. Brush with melted butter and bake in a moderate oven until crisp and well browned. Wrap in foil and pack at once in an insulated bag or leave to cool.

Makes about 10 crêpes

Crêpe Fillings:
Apple/Yogurt/Raisins
Apple/Cheese
Sliced oranges/
   Whipped cream/Sugar
Cream cheese/Lemon/Sugar

Ratatouille
Asparagus/Cheese
Cheese/Ham
Cheese/Bacon/Tomato

TERRINE DE CANARD

(Terrine of Duck)

6–8 rashers streaky bacon
8oz (225g) cooked duck meat
juice of half an orange
2 tablespoons brandy
8oz (225g) minced veal
1 small onion

8oz (225g) minced belly of
  pork
$\frac{1}{2}$ clove garlic
salt and pepper
2 bay leaves

$1\frac{1}{2}$lb (675g) loaf tin or terrine

Remove the skin and slice the duck meat thinly. Put into a bowl with the juice of half an orange and the brandy. Mix well, then leave for about 15 minutes or until almost all the juice has been absorbed (stir from time to time). In another bowl, put the minced veal and pork. Chop the onion finely, crush the garlic (half a small clove) in a small amount of salt and add both to the minced meats. Mix well, then add a generous sprinkling of

243

salt and pepper (this pâté needs to be well seasoned) and any of the juice not absorbed by the duck meat.

Stretch the bacon rashers with the back of a knife on a chopping board and use to line the loaf tin or terrine. Then put in a layer of the duck meat, one of minced meat, and then repeat the layers. Press two bay leaves on top and cover tightly with foil. Place the dish in a roasting tin filled with about an inch (2·5cm) of warm water. Cook in the centre of a preheated oven (350°F / Gas Mark 4 / 180°C) for about 1¼ hours (or until no pink juices run out of the pâté when pressed lightly with the back of a spoon). Take out, put several weights on top and leave to cool completely. Then cover with a lid or fresh piece of foil and pack. Or reverse the terrine out on to a plate, cover with foil or cling film and pack.

Serves 6–8

American Picnics

One of the chief contributions the Indians made to the cuisine of New England was the clambake. Later, New England clambakes, like Kentucky burgoos, were put on to attract voters to election rallies, and became the excuse for innumerable social outings. In the latter half of the nineteenth century, upper Narrangansett Bay in Rhode Island was crowded with clambake resorts like Rocky Point and Crescent Park. Bakes were served every day, and fleets of steamboats operating out of Providence and the neighbouring area ran excursions to these clambake sites along the shore.

from *The American Heritage Cookbook*

The picnic tradition is well established in America but varies considerably from one part of the country to another. While New England is famous for its clambakes, the Midwest prides itself on its barbecues and the South hosts the most elaborate 'cookouts' ever.

NEW ENGLAND PICNIC

Corn Chowder

***

Cold Turkey Sandwiches

Devilled Eggs

Tossed Salad

***

Pumpkin Pie
and
Whipped Cream

***

Chilled Cider

OKLAHOMA PICNIC

Barbecue Chicken

Coleslaw

Corn on the Cob

***

Banana Cake

***

Iced Tea

SOUTHERN PICNIC

Chicken Gumbo Soup

***

Shrimp Creole
with
Rice

Green Salad

***

Butter Pecan Ice-cream
and
Icebox Biscuits

***

Mint Julep or Iced Tea

ALL-AMERICAN PICNIC

Carrot and Celery Sticks
Crisps
and
Dips
(Roquefort, Onion or Bacon)

***

Spicy Meat Loaf

Potato Salad

***

Chocolate Cake

***

Iced Coffee

Consult the index for recipes for the above.

CHICKEN GUMBO SOUP

2 large chicken breasts
2 chicken stock cubes
2 pints (1·1 litres) boiling water
4oz (100g) okra
1 medium onion
1 small green pepper
2 large stalks celery
1oz (25g) butter
1 (14oz/400g) tin of tomatoes
1 bay leaf
salt and black pepper
1 tablespoon chopped parsley

Remove the skin from the chicken breasts, then put the chicken into a large saucepan. Dissolve the stock cubes in the boiling water, and add to the pan with a small bay leaf. Bring to the boil, then cover and simmer until the chicken is cooked through. Pour the liquid into a jug, take the chicken out and leave until cool enough to handle. Remove the bones and chop the flesh into small chunks.

Wash the okra well, then cut off the stem and slice horizontally. Peel the onion and chop finely. Remove the white pith and seeds from the pepper, then chop it and the celery into small dice. Melt the butter in a saucepan and, when foaming, add the chopped vegetables. Stir until well coated in the butter. Cook over moderate heat, shaking the pan occasionally, for about twenty minutes or until the vegetables are cooked through. Add the tomatoes and their juice, the chicken stock (skim any fat off first) and chicken chunks and a good sprinkling of salt and freshly ground black pepper. Bring to the boil, then reduce the heat and simmer uncovered for about an hour, stirring from time to time. Check the seasoning and adjust if necessary. Add the chopped parsley and pour into a warmed Thermos.

Serves 6

SHRIMP CREOLE

1oz (25g) butter
1 medium onion
1 green pepper
2 stalks celery
2 gammon rashers

1 garlic clove
1 (14oz/400g) tin of tomatoes
large pinch dried thyme
salt and pepper to taste
4oz–6oz (100g–175g) prawns

1 tablespoon chopped parsley

Cooked rice for 4 people

Melt the butter in a large heavy frying pan. Chop the onion finely, then cut the green pepper, celery and gammon rashers (remove the rind first) into small dice. Add to the pan with the crushed garlic clove. Cook over moderate heat, stirring frequently to prevent sticking, until the onion is soft but not coloured. Stir in the tomatoes with a pinch of dried thyme and a good sprinkling of salt and pepper. Reduce the heat and simmer for 10 minutes. Add the prawns, mix in well and cook for 10 minutes more. Then check the seasoning and adjust if necessary.

Line a preheated aluminium-foil container with hot cooked rice, then top with the creole. Sprinkle with chopped parsley, cover tightly with cardboard lid and pack at once in an insulated bag. This is at its best if served piping hot but if you would prefer to serve it cold, mix 1–2 tablespoons of olive oil into the rice and use it to line a plastic container. Stir ½–1 tablespoon of oil into the creole, spoon on top of the rice and sprinkle witn parsley. (Or the creole can be folded into the rice.) Cover with a lid and pack.

Serves 4

PUMPKIN PIE

6oz (175g) rich shortcrust pastry
1 (14oz/400g) tin of pumpkin
1 teaspoon ground cinnamon
1 teaspoon ground mixed spice
½ teaspoon ground ginger
½ teaspoon ground nutmeg
¼ teaspoon ground cloves
½ teaspoon salt
6oz (175g) brown sugar
2 large eggs
¼ pint (150ml) single cream
7oz (200ml) milk
2 tablespoons sherry (optional)

8″ (20cm) or 9″ (23cm) pie plate or dish
Preheat oven to 425°F / Gas Mark 7 / 220°C.

Roll out the pastry and use to line the pie dish. Trim and flute the edges, then chill until the filling is ready.

Put the pumpkin, spices, sugar and salt into a mixing bowl and stir until well blended. Beat the eggs lightly and mix with the cream, milk (and sherry if used). Then gently stir into the pumpkin mixture. Pour into the pie dish and bake in the centre of the oven for 15 minutes. Then reduce the heat to 350°F/ Gas Mark 4/180°C and bake for a further 45 minutes or until a knife inserted in the centre or side comes out clean. Cover with foil and pack, or leave to cool. Serve hot or cold with lightly whipped cream.

If making pumpkin tarts, fill lined patty tins almost to the top with the pumpkin mixture as it tends to shrink slightly as it cooks.

Serves 6–8

QUICK CHOCOLATE CAKE

4oz (100g) soft butter
10oz (275g) sugar
2 large eggs
2oz (50g) cocoa powder
1 teaspoon bicarbonate of soda
½ teaspoon baking powder
½ teaspoon salt
8oz (225g) plain flour
¾ teaspoon vanilla
8oz (225ml) water

Grease and lightly flour a 10" (25cm) spring-form tube pan,* or a deep 8" (20cm) cake tin, or 2 small sandwich tins.
Preheat oven to 350°F / Gas Mark 4 / 180°C.

Put all the ingredients into a very large mixing bowl with half the water. Mix, using an electric whisk, on low speed until well blended. Then gradually add the remaining water and when it has all been thoroughly mixed in, whisk on high speed for 2–3 minutes. Pour into prepared tin and bake in the centre of the oven for about 45 minutes or until a toothpick inserted in the centre comes out clean. Loosen round the outside edge (and inside edge, if using a tube pan) with a knife, then carefully reverse on to a wire rack. Leave the tin on for at least 10 minutes, then tap the top lightly all the way around and remove. Leave to cool completely, then sprinkle the top with caster or icing sugar, or cut in half horizontally and fill with chocolate icing. Pack in a large cake tin or round plastic container.

Makes 1 large cake

* Make sure that the base is in tightly and if at all doubtful, put the tin on a baking tray before it goes into the oven.

CHOCOLATE ICING

2oz (50g) dark chocolate (unsweetened)
2oz (50g) soft butter

4oz (100g) sifted icing sugar
1 teaspoon vanilla
2 tablespoons milk

Put the chocolate in a bowl or plate over hot water and leave until completely melted. Cool slightly, then put in a bowl with the butter, icing sugar, vanilla and milk. Blend with an electric whisk until light and fluffy, adding more milk if too thick or more icing sugar if not thick enough. Cut the cake in half horizontally and spread the bottom layer with icing. Replace the top, press into position and pack in a cake tin.

14
SPECIAL PICNICS

Brunch Picnics

'How quick your servants are!' Miss Quested exclaimed. For a cloth had already been laid, with a vase of artificial flowers in its centre, and Mahmoud Ali's butler offered them poached eggs and tea for the second time.

'I thought we would eat this before our caves, and breakfast after.'

'Isn't this breakfast?'

'This breakfast? Did you think I should treat you so strangely?' He had been warned that English people never stop eating, and that he had better nourish them every two hours until a solid meal was ready.

from *A Passage to India* by E. M. Forster

The great advantage of brunch picnics is that by combining two meals, you usually get the best of both. There is no urgency to eat at a specific time and, consequently, they have a relaxed, unhurried air about them.

SPRING BRUNCH PICNIC

Cranberry/Orange Cocktail

***

French Apple, Date and Asparagus Salad

Cold Sausages and Mustard

Granary Bread

***

Hungarian Coffee Cake

Hot Coffee

SUMMER BRUNCH PICNIC

(For hot weather and special occasions)

Buck's Fizz

Pâté-filled Croissants

***

Quiche Lorraine

Mixed Green Salad

***

Strawberries and Peaches Romanoff

Iced Coffee

AUTUMN BRUNCH PICNIC

Fresh Orange Juice

***

Bacon Buns

Devilled Eggs

Stuffed Tomatoes with Sausagemeat

Wheatmeal Scones

***

Blackberry Coffee Cake

Hot Spiced Tea

WINTER BRUNCH PICNIC

Orange-glazed Ham Slices

French Tomato Salad

Rice Salad with Onion and Bacon

***

Farmhouse Cheddar

Wholewheat Rolls

Apples and Grapes

***

Irish Coffee

The page numbers of these recipes can be found in the index.

STRAWBERRIES AND PEACHES ROMANOFF

8oz (225g) fresh strawberries
4 large ripe peaches

1 miniature bottle Cointreau
icing sugar

Medium bowl or plastic container

Wash and hull the strawberries, then drain well. Peel the peaches and slice thinly. Put both into a bowl and sprinkle with a small amount of icing sugar (this will depend on the sweetness of the fruit). Let stand for 5–10 minutes or until the sugar has dissolved. Pour over the Cointreau and mix carefully with two spoons. Fill a bowl or plastic container with the fruit, cover with lid or cling film and refrigerate until needed.

Serves 4

BLACKBERRY COFFEE CAKE (Quick)

9oz (250g) plain flour
6oz (175g) sugar
2½ teaspoons baking powder
¾ teaspoon salt
2oz (50g) butter, melted

1 large egg
5oz (150ml) milk
1 large (10oz/280g) tin
   blackberries

Topping:
3oz (75g) soft brown sugar
2oz (50g) plain flour

1 teaspoon ground cinnamon
2oz (50g) cold butter

Grease a 9" (23cm) square tin and line with greaseproof paper. Grease again.
Preheat oven to 350°F / Gas Mark 4 / 180°C.

Sift the flour, sugar, baking powder and salt into a large mixing bowl. Make a well in the centre, then pour in the melted butter, lightly beaten egg and milk. Draw the flour in gradually from around the sides and stir only until all the ingredients have been blended in. Then carefully fold in the blackberries and pour the mixture into the prepared tin.

To make the topping: Sift the flour into a bowl and mix in the sugar and cinnamon. Cut the butter into small pieces and rub in lightly until the mixture resembles coarse breadcrumbs. Sprinkle evenly over the batter in the tin. Bake in the centre of the preheated oven for an hour or until a toothpick inserted in the centre comes out clean. Lift the cake carefully out of the tin holding on to the greaseproof paper and leave to cool on a wire rack. Remove the paper and transfer to a cake tin, or cut in half and wrap each section in cling film. Serve sliced with butter. (If kept in a polythene bag or cling film, this cake will keep for 4 or 5 days.)

Makes 1 large cake

Railway Picnics

I well remember the first time I had a luncheon basket on a train; ordered ahead by wire it was brought to the carriage at some main-line station en route. Now, I thought, I really am grown up, no more packets of sandwiches for me. Someone must have tipped the guard, for I remember he brought in a fresh footwarmer and inquired if I was comfortable. Hair up, long skirts, luncheon basket, the *Strand* magazine, on my way to my first house party – I was beginning life. In the basket was a wing of chicken, roll, butter, biscuits, cheese, and, I think, celery and possibly cake or a jam tart and an apple, and I have an idea it cost 2*s* 6*d*, though it may have been less.

Constance Spry

It's difficult to relate the passage above to rail travel today which, though speedy and comfortable, is something of a gastronomic desert. Gone are the days of the *Orient Express* and first-rate restaurant cars; you would be lucky now to find a packet of sandwiches. Perhaps then we should revive the luncheon basket and while not expecting this to be delivered to your carriage, it could travel quite easily with the passenger. It could be packed at the same time as your suitcase and filled with a colourful 'potpourri' of foods. In the midst of them would be a Thermos of hot tea, soup or mulled cider, or perhaps a bottle of wine. And with the day's newspaper, a glossy magazine or paperback tucked down the side, the basket would be complete.

RAILWAY PICNIC FOR TWO

(Summer)

Boursin Biscuits

***

Lemon Chicken

Saffron Salad with Nuts and Raisins

***

Blackberry Mousse

***

Iced Coffee, Cider or Wine

NB: Use drumsticks for the chicken recipe so that they are easier to eat, and pack the salad in individual containers so that you don't need plates.

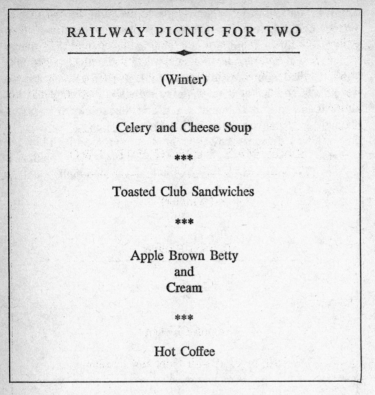

RAILWAY PICNIC FOR TWO

(Winter)

Celery and Cheese Soup

***

Toasted Club Sandwiches

***

Apple Brown Betty
and
Cream

***

Hot Coffee

Consult the index for recipes for the above. (Quantities will need to be reduced proportionately.)

Seaside Picnics

Sand in the sandwiches, wasps in the tea,
Sun on our bathing-dresses, heavy with the wet,
Squelch of the bladder-wrack waiting for the sea,
Fleas round the tamarisk, an early cigarette.

Sir John Betjeman from his *Selected Poems*

Sand in the sandwiches is almost a pre-requisite of seaside picnics and keeping it to a minimum quantity requires a concentrated effort. After a morning lying in the sun and the lethargy which inevitably sets in, the cry will be for light, refreshing food. Chilled soups, sandwiches, cold chicken pieces, stuffed vegetables and ice-creams are easy to eat and perfect for hot days. If the soup is served in mugs and the ice-cream in cones, then the rest can be eaten with fingers. (Fewer plates seem to mean fewer disasters and less sand in the food.) Fill a tall Thermos with ice-cold punch and a short food flask with ice-cubes. This will satisfy those who find they haven't even the energy to eat!

SEASIDE PICNIC FOR TWO

Stuffed Cucumbers

***

Individual 'Pan Bagna'

Cherry Tomatoes

***

Caribbean Grape Dessert

***

Chilled White Wine

SEASIDE PICNIC FOR FOUR

Chilled Tomato and Orange Soup

***

Spring Onion and Cress Tartlets

Carrot and Celery Sticks

***

Snow Pudding

and

Sponge Cake or Biscuits

***

Summer Fruit Punch

CHILDREN'S SEASIDE PICNICS

Cocktail Sausages and Mustard

***

Egg Salad Sandwiches

Tuna Sandwiches

Peanut Butter Sandwiches

***

Orange Pineapple Ice-cream

Biscuits or Brownies

***

Lemonade

Consult the index for recipes for the above. (The quantities will need to be reduced proportionately.)

Skytrain Picnics

Now that Freddie Laker has made 'impromptu' travelling so easy, we need picnics to match. And however tempting it might be to take just a sandwich and an apple, they won't last long on a seven-hour flight! To combat boredom and hunger pangs, a well-filled 'picnic bag' is the answer.

As pre-flight preparations always seem to have an element of rush to them, all the food below can be made the day before. When deciding what to take, avoid foods that are salty (or, alternatively, take lots to drink). Pack the food, if possible, in individual plastic containers so that you don't need plates (or use paper ones). Margarine, cottage cheese and yogurt tubs are ideal because they can be thrown away afterwards. But do make sure they have tightly fitting lids. Covering them with foil or cling film is only inviting disaster. If using a plastic carrier-bag to put the food in, be sure to pack it vertically so that it is kept the right way up. Put the heavy things at the bottom so that it is properly balanced. Shopping lists are given so that no precious time is wasted trying to remember what you've forgotten.

PICNIC FOR 1

---◆---

Pâté

Melba Toast

***

Chinese Meatballs

Sweetcorn and Spring Onion Salad

***

Camembert

Green or Black Grapes

***

Wine or Chilled Cider

*Shopping List:**

slice of pâté
4–5 slices bread
butter
½lb (225g) lean minced beef
3 spring onions

1–2 triangles Camembert
½lb (225g) grapes
½ bottle wine or tin of chilled cider
dried onion flakes

* assuming that the larder already contains salt, pepper, vinegar, olive or vegetable oil, Worcestershire sauce, French mustard, 1 egg, absorbent kitchen paper, foil, plastic or aluminium-foil containers with lids.

tomato ketchup   plastic glass or paper cup
honey   paper plate
brown sugar   polythene bags
1 small tin sweetcorn   paper napkins

Preparation:

(1) Follow the recipe for Chinese meatballs given on page 127, dividing the quantities in half (or more, depending on your appetite). Use a very small egg or half a large one.

(2) While the meatballs are cooking, open the tin of sweetcorn, drain well and put into a bowl. Wash the spring onions, top and tail them, then slice finely. Add to the sweetcorn. Put ½ teaspoon French mustard, ½ teaspoon brown sugar, 1 tablespoon vinegar, 3 tablespoons olive or vegetable oil, salt and pepper into a screw-top jar. Shake vigorously until well blended then pour over the salad and mix well. Season well with salt and pepper and transfer to a small plastic container.

(3) Wash the grapes and dry well in absorbent kitchen paper. Then put into a polythene bag.

(4) Cut off a small portion of butter (to use with the pâté and the cheese) and wrap in a piece of foil. Wrap the remaining butter in foil and put in the refrigerator (it will keep for 3–4 weeks).

(5) Take the meatballs out of the oven and leave to cool, then put into a small plastic or aluminium container or wrap in foil.

(6) Remove the crusts, then put 3 or 4 slices of bread on a baking tray and into the oven (325°F / Gas Mark 3 / 170°C) and leave until crisp and lightly browned. Cool, then pack in a polythene bag.

(7) Pack the meatballs and sweetcorn salad at the bottom of the carrier-bag with a fork, knife, corkscrew (wrapped in a paper napkin), paper plate and plastic or paper cup. Pack the wine or cider along the side, then wrap the pâté well and put on top with the melba toast, butter, Camembert and grapes.

PICNIC FOR 2

Crudités and Onion Dip

***

Chicken Côte D'Or

Orange and Celery Salad

Rolls and Butter

***

Fruit Salad

Biscuits

***

Wine

Shopping List:*

½lb (225g) carrots
small bunch celery (6 stalks)
½ small cucumber
1 packet dried onion soup mix
5oz (150ml) carton sour cream

butter
2 apples
3 oranges
¼lb (100g) grapes
1 lemon

* this is assuming that the larder already contains salt, pepper, mayonnaise, vinegar, sherry, polythene bags, foil, paper napkins.

thick honey	biscuits
Dijon mustard	rolls
sugar	bottle of wine
4 chicken pieces	paper cups or plastic glasses
	paper plates

Preparation:

(1) Follow the recipe for Chicken Côte D'or (check the index for the page number), dividing the quantities in half.

(2) Peel the carrots and cut into julienne strips. Wash and dry the cucumber, then cut into thin strips. Wash the celery, slice 2 stalks into thin strips and cut 4 stalks into dice.

(3) Put the diced celery into a bowl and add 2 oranges, peeled and sliced thinly. Put 1 teaspoon Dijon mustard, 1 teaspoon sugar, 1 tablespoon of vinegar and 4–5 tablespoons mayonnaise into a small jar. Shake vigorously until blended, then season to taste with salt and pepper. Pour over the salad, toss well, then transfer to a plastic container.

(4) Wash and dry the apples, then cut into small chunks. Peel the remaining orange and slice thinly. Put these into a bowl with the chopped apples and the grapes which have been washed, halved and the pips removed. Pour over the juice of half a lemon and sweeten to taste with sugar. Add a tablespoon of sherry or kirsch if you have it, mix well and put into a plastic container. Pack the biscuits in a polythene bag.

(5) Mix the sour cream with half the onion soup mix and pour into a small container. Put the crudités into a strong polythene bag with a sprinkling of crushed ice and tie tightly. Cool the chicken on a rack, then sprinkle with salt and pepper and wrap in foil. Butter the rolls and put in a polythene bag. Pack all the food in a strong carrier-bag. (Don't forget to pack forks, knives, spoons, corkscrew, paper napkins, paper plates and glasses.)

Barbecue Picnics

Dickon made the stimulating discovery that in the wood in the park outside the garden where Mary had first found him piping to the wild creatures, there was a deep little hollow where you could build a sort of tiny oven with stones and roast potatoes and eggs in it. Roasted eggs were a previously unknown luxury, and very hot potatoes with salt and fresh butter in them were fit for a woodland king – besides being deliciously satisfying.

from *The Secret Garden*

The great interest in barbecues in the past few years has produced a vast range of new equipment. The only problem now is deciding which to use! For smaller picnics, the Japanese Hibachi is probably the most practical as it can be easily stowed in the back of a car (or on a bicycle). The larger hooded or brazier types are more difficult to transport and are best suited to picnics in the back garden. A compromise between the two is the small 'picnic' barbecue which is quite low to the ground and has a circular revolving grill. It's easy to use and to pack. If none of the above are available, you can always resort to a large biscuit-tin with holes punched in the sides and a piece of chicken wire (or fine mesh wire) on top.

The most important thing to get right at a barbecue is the timing. Food should be cooked over glowing coals and it takes 20–45 minutes after the fire is lit for them to reach this stage. Always have a bucket of sand or water near the barbecue in case the fire gets out of control.

Most meats have a better flavour and are more tender if

marinated for several hours before grilling. (Recipes for several of these are given.) Brush the meat with melted butter or vegetable oil before putting on the grill. Some marinades can be used as basting sauces and these can be brushed on with a sprig of rosemary or a pastry brush. If the basting sauce contains tomato, only baste for the last 10 minutes of cooking. Some foods which require longer cooking (e.g. spareribs, corn) can be precooked in the oven or on top of the stove and then finished off on the barbecue.

Barbecue Foods

Lamb or Pork Chops
Steaks
Hamburgers
Sausages
Frankfurters

Spareribs
Chicken
Toasted Sandwiches
Shish-kebabs

WRAPPED IN FOIL

Potatoes
Corn
Fish

Garlic or Herb Bread
Pineapple

SHISH-KEBAB SUGGESTIONS

Pork/apple/sausage
Chicken/bacon/mushroom/
  tomato

Liver/bacon/tomato/onion
Lamb/green pepper/onion/
  tomato

Essential equipment:
Charcoal
Methylated spirit
Matches
Firelighters (just in case)

Long fork
Oven gloves
Torch (for evening barbecues)
Damp j-cloths

MARINADE FOR CHICKEN OR LAMB

3oz (75ml) olive or vegetable oil
3oz (75ml) white wine
juice of half a lemon
½ teaspoon dried rosemary

1 small onion, finely chopped
1 teaspoon salt
¼ teaspoon black pepper
large pinch sugar

Put all the ingredients into a clean coffee-jar and shake vigorously until well blended. Check the seasoning and adjust if necessary. Then pour over the chicken or lamb and leave for several hours in a cool place (spoon the mixture over the meat from time to time). Use a fresh sprig of rosemary to baste the meat with the marinade while cooking.

MARINADE FOR BEEF/LAMB/PORK

1 small onion
1 clove garlic (optional)
4oz (100ml) red wine
3oz (75ml) olive or vegetable oil

1oz (25ml) red wine vinegar
½ teaspoon French mustard
large pinch sugar
large pinch dried basil or oregano

salt and pepper to taste

Chop the onion finely and crush the garlic to a paste in a small amount of salt. Put these and the remaining ingredients into a clean coffee-jar. Shake vigorously until well blended. Check the seasoning and adjust if necessary. Pour over the meat and leave in a cool place for several hours (basting the meat with the mixture from time to time). Then transfer the meat to the barbecue and use the marinade to baste it as it cooks.

BARBECUE SAUCE

The meat must only be basted with this sauce for the final part of the cooking; otherwise it will have a bitter flavour and will most likely burn.

8 tablespoons tomato ketchup
2 tablespoons lemon juice
2 teaspoons Worcestershire
   sauce

2 tablespoons water
3 tablespoons brown sugar
½ teaspoon French mustard
salt and pepper to taste

Put all the ingredients into a bowl and mix until well blended. Check the seasoning and adjust if necessary. Use to baste chicken, lamb or pork chops for the last 10 minutes of cooking.

GARLIC BREAD

Always a favourite, indoors or out.

1 long French loaf
4oz butter, at room
   temperature

2–3 cloves garlic
salt

Slice the bread diagonally from the top down to the bottom crust, being careful not to cut through it. Crush the garlic cloves to a paste in a generous amount of salt. Soften the butter in a bowl and gradually blend in the garlic. Then use to spread one side of each slice in the loaf. Wrap tightly in foil and put on top of the barbecue, turning at regular intervals. Leave over the fire until piping hot.

ROAST CORN

Prepare the corn by pulling the husks back and removing the 'silk' which forms a layer inside. Then rub the corn with soft butter, put the husks back in place and wrap in foil. Bury in the coals or cook on top of the barbecue, turning frequently. It will take 20–30 minutes but this varies with the heat of the barbecue.

Recipes for the following, which can also be cooked on a barbecue, are given in the chapter on Meat/Chicken/Fish Dishes: Chicken with Barbecue Sauce; Trout 'en Papillote'; Grilled Mullet; Stuffed Bass or Trout; Spareribs with Ginger and Honey.

Camping Picnics

They came back to camp wonderfully refreshed, glad-hearted and ravenous; and they soon had the camp-fire blazing again . . . While Joe was slicing bacon for breakfast, Tom and Huck asked him to hold on a minute; they stepped to a promising nook in the river bank and threw in their lines; almost immediately they had reward. Joe had not had time to get impatient before they were back again with some handsome bass, a couple of sun-perch and a small cat-fish – provision enough for quite a family. They fried the fish with the bacon and were astonished; for no fish had ever seemed so delicious before.

from *The Adventures of Tom Sawyer*

If the weather is fine, there is nothing to beat cooking over an open fire. Even the simplest foods taste and smell better than ever before. But it's not always as easy as it looks. It *is* important to have the right equipment and cater for all eventualities (particularly those involving the weather). Some things (i.e. scone dough, pancake batter) can be half-prepared before leaving, then mixed and cooked at the camp-site.

PICNIC BREAKFAST

Fresh Oranges

***

Bacon, Eggs, Sausages

Toast and Jam
or
French Toast and Maple Syrup

***

Hot Coffee and Tea

PICNIC LUNCH

Toasted Cheese Sandwiches

or

Frankfurters wrapped in bacon
with buns

***

Apples

Oatmeal Flapjacks

***

Hot Coffee and Tea

PICNIC SUPPER

Tomato Soup
(made from a packet)

***

Thin 'minute' steaks

Roast Corn

Baked Potatoes

***

Lemon Biscuit Pie
or
Toasted Marshmallows

Basic Equipment:
Newspapers (to help start the fire)
Firelighters (ditto)
Matches
Kindling
Long toasting forks
Heavy frying pan
Saucepan or pot with handle
Fish slice
Oven glove
Soap
Tea towel

Basic Supplies:
Milk – dried or fresh
Eggs – dried or fresh
Coffee, tea, cocoa
Salt and pepper
Sugar
Mustard
Bread
Bacon
Sausages
Cheese
Apples, oranges, bananas
Biscuits

Foil
Plates, cups, bowls, cutlery
Pie tin
Hatchet
Pen-knife
Tin-opener/corkscrew
Aluminium coffee and/or
  tea pot
Wooden spoon
Torch

Jam
Butter
Packet soup
Baked beans
Water (if no drinking water
  available)

Camping Picnic Tips

***** Take care when choosing a spot for the fire that it is away from overhanging branches and thick tree roots.

***** Always place a bucket of water or sand within easy reach in case the fire gets out of control (especially if there is a strong wind). Douse the fire when you leave with *lots* of water and sand.

***** If toasting forks are unavailable, then use green saplings. Strip off the side branches and sharpen to a point at one end. Use to toast bread, marshmallows and sausages.

***** Remember that it will take 30 minutes to an hour after the fire has been lit to produce hot coals to cook over.

***** To make washing easier, soap the bottom of all the pans generously before using (a thick bar of household soap is best).

***** Dig a trench round the fire before lighting to prevent any tree roots catching fire.

***** Build up the fire with dry leaves and twigs placed wigwam fashion in the centre, with bigger branches in a log cabin around it. Only add the logs once the fire is going nicely. Good ventilation is crucial.

***** If using a frying pan or skillet, it can be rested on a grill standing over the fire or on several logs (placed in a triangle over the fire).

***** Make sure your wood is dry or the fire will smoke badly. Split the wood open first: even though wet outside, the centre may still be dry.

Camping Food

BREAKFAST:

The bacon and eggs can be cooked easily in a frying pan over the fire. The bread can be toasted on green sticks or toasting forks. Boil the water for coffee or tea in a large saucepan or pot with a handle.

FRENCH TOAST

4–6 slices bread	large pinch of salt
2 large eggs	4oz (100ml) milk
	butter for frying

Mix the eggs lightly with a fork or whisk, then add the salt and blend in the milk. Dip each slice of bread into the batter and fry on both sides until golden brown. Serve hot with maple syrup or sprinkled with sugar and lemon (or cinnamon).

Lunch

TOASTED CHEESE SANDWICHES

8 slices of bread	4 slices of processed cheese
	soft butter

Butter one side of each slice of bread, then put together with a slice of cheese between two of bread, buttered side out. Melt a small amount of butter in a frying pan and fry the sandwiches until golden brown (adding more butter if necessary). Eat at once.

Makes 4 sandwiches

FRANKFURTERS WRAPPED IN BACON

6 frankfurters
6 streaky bacon rashers

6 long finger rolls
soft butter
mustard

Wrap each frankfurter with a rasher of bacon and secure with a toothpick (or a small green twig, stripped of bark and sharpened at one end). Slide carefully (lengthwise) on to a green stick or (widthwise) on to a toasting fork. Grill over the fire until the bacon is cooked. Butter the buns and spread the inside of one half with mustard, if you like. Put a cooked frankfurter into each one and serve at once.

Serves 4–6

OATMEAL FLAPJACKS

6oz (175g) quick-cooking oats
4oz (100g) soft brown sugar

3oz (75g) butter
2oz (50ml) golden syrup

Measure out the oats and brown sugar before leaving and pack together in a polythene bag. Measure the butter and golden syrup and put these into a small plastic container with a tightly fitting lid (also pack a spatula to get them out with). When ready to cook, melt the butter and syrup in a frying pan over the fire. Then add the oats and brown sugar, mix thoroughly, then press evenly over the base of the pan with the back of a spoon. Cover with foil and put over the fire (in a spot where there is even heat). Cook for 10–15 minutes (check frequently as this depends on the heat of the fire) or until the underside is well browned. Take off the heat and cut into triangles. Leave for 5 minutes, then lift carefully out of the pan and on to a plate. Cool completely, then serve with fresh fruit.

Makes 8 large flapjacks

Supper

Make up the soup following the instructions on the packet. Precook the corn in boiling water for about 3 minutes, then wrap in foil and roast for a further 10–15 minutes or until done (or, if you prefer, cook completely in the hot water). Wrap the potatoes in foil and bury in the coals. These will take 45 minutes to an hour depending on the size of the potato and the heat of the fire.

LEMON BISCUIT PIE

8 digestive biscuits
5 tablespoons butter
2 tablespoons sugar

1 small (2½oz/70g) packet lemon pie filling
1 egg
9oz (250ml) drinking water

Put the digestive biscuits into a polythene bag and crush to crumbs with a small stone. Add the sugar and shake in the bag to mix well. Melt the butter in a frying pan (or a pie tin) over the fire. Take off the heat and add the biscuit crumbs. Mix well with a wooden spoon, then press an even layer over the base and half-way up the sides of the pan. Put over the fire again for about 5 minutes, then remove and leave to cool. Empty the contents of the lemon pie filling packet into a saucepan or pot with a handle. Separate the egg and add the yolk and drinking water to the pan. Mix well, then cook over the fire until the mixture boils and thickens, stirring frequently. Then take off the heat and pour into the biscuit crust. Put to one side until quite cold and completely set. Then cut into triangles and lift out carefully with a fish slice.

Serves 6

INDEX